# Kenya

Jarrold Publishing

# CONTENTS

*Title page: Masai and dwellings*

*Lions in Masai Mara*

# Introduction to Kenya

Had Johann Ludwig Krapf, first European to penetrate to the very heart of Kenya, had more of an ear for the native language, the country today would almost certainly be known as *Kirinyaga*, for that is the Kikuyu name of the 5,000-m-high 'black mountain flecked with white' that the German missionary caught sight of for the first time on December 3rd 1849.

Krapf's mistake was hardly important at the time. Back home in Europe people found his tale of snow and ice on the equator too comical for belief. Kenya – as he called the mountain – came to symbolise little more than a wild flight of fancy and the existence of a land of dreams.

Today Krapf's misunderstanding has long been forgotten. Kenya is a reality, though in its way dreamlike all the same. Its people have long since become used to the abbreviated name, just as they have become used to the preconceptions and oversimplifications that visitors often bring to the country. It has to be said, however, that Kenya does not make things easy for newcomers either. It is a confusing country, full of contradictions. It is a country that has everything, but is above all a place of contrasts. It is a land of lakes and dry savannahs, of deserts and forests, of tropical beaches and permanent ice.

More than forty different peoples make up Kenya's multi-faceted society, which includes town-dwellers, farmers and nomads. A Kenyan may be a computer expert or a Masai herdsman, who, game laws notwithstanding, will kill a lion with his spear to prove his courage. A Kenyan may just as easily be an Arab trader or a farmer who trusts in the power of a buffalo horn to ward off evil.

Those who visit Kenya can be every bit as various. Some choose to holiday there intent on enjoying real luxury; others – whether they are mountaineers or diving

*Watersports facilities, Diani Beach, Mombasa*

enthusiasts — come in search of real adventure. Some arrive filled with the self-assurance of people who have seen it all before; others come brimming with curiosity, with everything to learn.

The Chinese have a saying that no one steps into the same river twice. It is true of Kenya that no two people ever find it quite the same. Each visitor's experience is unique, and those who come back again find themselves in a different country. Some may be taught the true meaning of 'tropical' by the torrid equatorial heat, while on that very same equator others may shiver and reach for a hotwater-bottle. On safari some may find themselves breathing enough dust to last a lifetime, while others may find their route cut off by a sea of water with the sudden and unexpected arrival of the rains. Journeying overland from Mombasa to Nairobi some may find the road mile after mile of endlessly boring sun-scorched bush, while others making the same journey a few days later may be transfixed by the sight of greenery stretching as far as the eye can see, ablaze with exotic flowers. And while one visitor may suffer the distress of having his wallet stolen, another, beset perhaps by a flat tyre and confronted by a herd of wild buffalo, will find no shortage of brave helpers quickly to hand.

Kenya, in other words, is the whole world in microcosm, with all its magnificence and all its problems. But this is an African world where time in particular is regarded in a way that visitors find difficult to understand. The Kenyans have a revealing expression in Swahili, their national tongue: they call Europeans *wazungu* — people who move restlessly from one place to another, people who never seem to have the time really to stop and look, to join in, or to stay.

## Essential details in brief

**Name:** Jamhuri ya Kenya (Republic of Kenya).

**Independence:** December 12th 1963.

**Area:** 582,644 sq km (Iberian Peninsula – Spain and Portugal – 580,000 sq km).

**Population:** About 20 million.
Density: 31 per sq km.
Annual growth rate: 3.9%.

**Official languages:** Swahili *(Kiswahili)* and English have equal status.

**Religion:** Christianity (c. 60%), Islam, Hinduism, traditional African religions.

**Capital:** Nairobi (pop. 1 million).

**Form of government:** Presidential democracy; constitutionally a one-party state since 1983.

**Political party:** KANU (Kenya African National Union).

**Parliament:** 158 elected members and 12 appointed by the President.

**Administrative divisions:** Seven provinces (Nairobi; Central, Coast, Eastern, North-eastern and Western Provinces; the Rift Valley).

**National flag:** Black, red and green with shield and crossed spears.

**Base economy:** Agriculture (coffee, tea, vegetables and flowers for export, maize and beans for home consumption); tourism; oil-processing.

**Major trade partners:** The United Kingdom, Germany and other countries of the EC.

**Economic growth:** About 3% per annum (GNP).

**Currency:** Kenyan shilling (KSh). 1 KSh = 100 cents.

**Local time:** GMT + 3 hours (9 am London = 12 noon Nairobi). For the period of British Summer Time: BST + 2 hours.

**Holidaying in Kenya**

Today's holidaymakers have one thing in common with the explorers of long ago: their first port of call is always Mombasa. Afterwards they will follow their differing inclinations. Some will choose not to stray too far from the beaches that flank the city on either side. Others, having spent a while in Mombasa, will set off into the interior on safari. Generally speaking a visit to Kenya offers far too much to spend all the time sunbathing. Even those who venture little outside the confines of their hotel complex are guaranteed to find themselves in dream surroundings. In Kenya it is the easiest thing in the world for visitors to find whatever suits them. Tourism is so well organised here that a holiday can be tailor-made for almost anyone.

Though offering everything the holidaymaker could wish for, Kenya has not lost its own character. A cautious approach to hotel architecture has cleverly blended African style with European comfort, and despite the continuous stream of new hotels under construction, holidaymakers do not yet find themselves hemmed in by concrete. The beaches are relatively empty and the sea still clean. All the usual kinds of sport are, of course, available: snorkelling, diving, surfing, sailing and deep-sea fishing, as well as golf and tennis. But even these are not enough to satisfy everyone. One tourist in two goes on safari, to experience a natural world that is untamed and unpredictable. Here it is mankind who bends to Nature's will, not the other way round.

Those intending to travel independently in Kenya should brief themselves fully before leaving home. For those who have neither the time nor the inclination to make their own arrangements, there is no shortage of safari operators. There is certainly no need to trust to chance meetings on the beach or in the street. *Karibuni Kenya* is the Swahili welcome with which you will frequently be greeted. It means 'come up close'. It is a charming invitation however you choose to take it up, whether by plane, rail, bus or Land Rover.

If you have set your sights on seeing the 'big five' (elephant, rhinoceros, lion, leopard and buffalo), choose the *Amboseli, Masai Mara, Tsavo* and *Samburu* National Parks. Those with more of an ornithological interest will find themselves enthralled by the birdlife of Lakes *Naivasha, Nakuru, Baringo* and *Bogoria*. And if you need an imposing backdrop for your photographic safari, you can animal-watch on the slopes of *Mount Kenya* and the *Aberdares*.

Highly recommended for the more active and adventurous are the climb up *Mount Kenya*, hill walking in the *Aberdares*, and the drive to *Lake Turkana*. You can also get to know the country by camel and on horseback, or on foot accompanied by an Askari guide.

Nowadays only game birds can be shot for sport. Kenya is trying to enforce a strict code of nature conservation. Many a former big-game hunter has turned to guiding tourists on photographic safaris, expeditions that can often be just as exclusive as in colonial times. And if you would like your holiday experience to include a very special glimpse of African culture, then head for the little island of *Lamu* and an insight into Swahili life as it once was.

Trips to *Tanzania* are a natural complement to any visit to Kenya. After seven years during which Tanzania kept its frontier with Kenya closed, safaris are gradually becoming possible once again.

*A 'working' Samburu visits his family*

Children, by the way, are made very welcome in Kenya. Since the Kenyans themselves often have large families, they have a wealth of practical understanding too. Hotels usually charge less than half price for children under twelve. A hungry eleven-year-old will still get a full-size meal despite the reduction.

## Every kind of landscape on earth

So what *would* you like to see? Lush tropical coastline or hostile lava fields, fertile farmland or endless dry savannah, glaciers at the head of high-lying alpine valleys or dense tropical rain forest? Travelling through Kenya is like journeying through every type of landscape on earth.

The *Great Rift Valley*, which stretches from Djibouti to Tanzania, is completely unsurpassed as a region of geological interest. Here you are actually present at the birth of an ocean that will grow to the size of the Atlantic – though it will take an estimated hundred million years before it is quite that big! The mighty massifs of Mounts *Kilimanjaro, Kenya* and *Elgon* bear striking witness to the area's volcanic activity, by no means confined to the past. Just over an hour's drive from Nairobi you can find hot springs gushing from the ground (and now being harnessed to provide electricity).

The floor of the Great Rift Valley is covered with shallow lakes that have no outlets and look like 'normal' lakes only from a distance. Most are fed by hot springs; their waters have a high salt or soda content and their levels change constantly. From time to time some of these lakes dry out completely. In remote antiquity the water-levels of Lakes Turkana and Naivasha are known to have been as much as 170 m higher than at present.

# 🪖 Signposts of history

**1.5 million years BC:** *Homo habilis* is living near Lake Turkana.

**About 2,000 years ago:** The Nilotics arrive from the Sudan, settling in East Africa. Ivory is exported to Rome.

**9th c. AD:** The caliphs of Baghdad establish trading settlements on the coast.

**12th–15th c:** The Swahili culture of the coast reaches its zenith. The Bantu arrive from the west and north.

**1498:** Vasco da Gama breaks his great voyage at Malindi.

**1505:** The Portuguese sack Mombasa.

**1593–6:** The Portuguese build Fort Jesus in Mombasa.

**1699:** Mombasa is taken by the Arabs.

**1846:** The earliest missionaries land in Mombasa. Two German missionaries, Rebmann and Krapf, become the first Europeans to set eyes on Mounts Kilimanjaro (1848) and Kenya (1849).

**1890:** With the Zanzibar–Heligoland Treaty, Britain and Germany mark out their respective spheres of influence in Africa.

**1895:** Kenya becomes a British Protectorate (East African Protectorate). Until independence in 1963, the coast remains in the possession of the Sultan of Zanzibar though held by Britain under lease.

**1896–1902:** The Uganda railway is constructed from Mombasa to Kampala. Nairobi is founded. Indians migrate from the subcontinent to Kenya.

**1903–6:** The Kenyan highlands become the 'white man's country', modelled on South Africa.

**1920:** The Protectorate becomes a British Crown Colony and is named Kenya. At the same time resistance to British rule re-emerges.

**1952–5:** The Mau Mau revolt brings serious disruption to Kenya.

**1957:** The process of constitutional reform begins.

**1963:** Kenya achieves independence. Jomo Kenyatta becomes the first president.

**1977:** The frontier between Kenya and Tanzania is closed.

**1978:** Kenyatta dies and is succeeded by Daniel T. arap Moi.

**1983:** Kenya, Uganda and Tanzania agree on closer co-operation. The frontier with Tanzania is reopened.

#  Phases of history

True to the principle that 'anything we do not know about does not exist', Europeans for a long time refused to acknowledge that Africa had any history prior to their 'discovery' of the continent. The myth of a 'continent without a history' has now been well and truly exploded. The fact is that, apart from the coastal strip, European interest in East Africa came really very late, at a time when the Europeans were intent on colonialisation.

Indeed, it was not until about 1850 that missionaries first penetrated into the Kenyan interior. Those who did so represented all shades of Christian belief and imparted an astonishing variety of creeds to the Kenyans. Missionaries were followed by explorers, merchants and soldiers. By 1880 a certain amount had come to be known about Kenya, but for quite a while longer the country remained little more than an obstacle to the British on the route to Uganda. It was not until 1895 that the Kenya of today was taken over by the British as the *East African Protectorate*, following Germany's involvement in what is now Tanzania.

*Jomo Kenyatta's statue, Nairobi*

Conditions in Kenya changed dramatically when construction of the Uganda railway was begun in 1896. Thousands of Indians were brought into the country as labourers. After completing their contracts they stayed on to build a commercial structure that is still crucial today. At the same time, more and more Europeans discovered the Kenyan highlands, superb country for settlers. Kenya suddenly became for many a land of unlimited opportunity.

## Utopian schemes

In 1894 a group of Utopian socialists came together on the island of Lamu towards the northern end of the Kenyan coast. They were followers of Theodor Herzl, author and editor of the *Wiener Allgemeine Zeitung* (a Viennese newspaper), whose vision of a Utopian society they planned to realise in Kenya. The project did not, however, go according to plan, and the group was soon split by internal wrangling. They left the people of Lamu with an enduring and negative picture of the European way of life.

Much more serious was a plan to resettle in Kenya oppressed Jews from eastern Poland and Russia. In 1903 the then British Colonial Secretary, Joseph Chamberlain, who was sympathetic to Zionism, made the movement a concrete offer – the free gift of 5,000 sq miles of land, together with complete self-government under a Jewish governor and total religious freedom. While Theodor Herzl, founder of Zionism, dreamed of creating an 'antechamber to the Holy Land' that he likened to the 'wilderness in which the followers of Moses passed forty years in preparation for settling in Canaan', the British settlers who were already established took action against these potential new arrivals. A three-man Jewish delegation that visited Kenya in 1904 was deliberately intimidated. The settlers arranged for them to meet fierce-looking Masai warriors, and regaled them with stories of man-eating lions. Eventually the delegation concluded that Kenya was unsuitable for settlement by Jewish immigrants, and the offer was declined with thanks by a majority of the Zionists. The settlers had won their battle and were to make sure that they won many more.

## 'White man's country'

Modelling itself on South Africa, Kenya became 'white man's country'. The Africans were quickly deprived of their land, while a tax on their huts forced them to hire themselves out as labourers to raise the wherewithal to pay.

The white settlers achieved their greatest gains during the First World War. London amply rewarded them for carrying on the fight against German forces in what was then German East Africa. Indians were prohibited from settling in the 'White Highlands'; Africans needed special permits to enter the lands from which they had been driven; and the scandalous practice of assigning 999-year leases on land (instead of the customary 99 years) was legalised.

In London, however, attitudes were gradually changing. Press and Parliament were against suppression of the African population, and British experience in Ghana had shown that production was cheaper with African labour than with European. But the small number of white settlers were still powerful enough to maintain their hold on Kenyan affairs. Social and economic differences and tribal conflicts created by the colonial system were not resolved until after the Second World War.

## The Mau Mau movement

From 1946 onwards organised resistance to the British began to emerge, mainly among the largest tribe, the Kikuyu. The rebels were sworn to the cause, taking the oath in secret ceremonies. The first attacks made the white settlers uneasy; then in 1952 a full state of emergency was declared. All of a sudden one name, *Mau Mau,* was on everybody's lips.

Media reports in Europe portrayed the Mau Mau as bloodthirsty savages. Official statistics, on the other hand, tell a rather different story: 32 white settlers, 63 white members of the security forces, and 2,000 Africans on the government side were killed in the freedom fighting. Among the Mau Mau, 11,500 Kenyans lost their lives, and 90,000 Mau Mau supporters were interned for up to ten years. All political organisations were banned.

By 1955 the Mau Mau were to all intents and purposes defeated. Public opinion in Britain, however, as well as among some Britons in Kenya, had begun to accept that the future of the country could not be left exclusively in the hands of the European settlers. The idea of a multiracial state was floated. If European influence was to continue at all, the settlers would have to make concessions. Little by little Kenya's Africans gained a greater say in their affairs. The fact that all political organisations had been banned by the British made things difficult initially for the African nationalists. Unresolved tribal differences became apparent at several conferences before Kenya was granted independence on December 12th 1963. By then Jomo Kenyatta ('the pearl' in the language of the Kikuyu) had already been President for six months.

## Independent Kenya

Kenyatta, a legend in his own lifetime, had not been an unchallenged leader from the outset. Others turned him into one during his years in internment. Under his presidency (1964–78), the Kikuyu further consolidated their position of power. They were also the chief beneficiaries of the land distribution that followed the departure of the white settlers.

Kenyatta preserved the institutions of the State largely as he found them. Although now in the hands of Kenyans, the colonial system of administration was retained, as was the British school system. Traffic continued to drive on the left, and the new African upper classes enjoyed British-style club life. Most important of all, Kenyatta did nothing to undermine the capitalist economy he had inherited. Even today Kenya's trade unions remain too weak to bring about any redress of social imbalances.

Following Kenyatta's death in 1978, the transfer of power to Daniel T. arap Moi, Kenyatta's vice-president, was unexpectedly smooth. With his Nyayo philosophy of peace, love and unity ('nyayo' means footprint and symbolises a policy of following in Kenyatta's footsteps), Moi's primary appeal is to the *wananchi,* the 'simple people'. They respect him first and foremost for standing firm against corruption and bureaucratic unfairness. Above all Moi, a non-Kikuyu, represents equality among the Kenyan tribes. An attempted coup by the Air Force on August 8th 1982 was quelled after only a few hours.

## The former show-piece of East Africa

Kenya was for a long time considered the show-piece of East Africa. Since then its reputation has considerably diminished. Even so, the country is still indisputably better off than all its neighbours.

Kenya has staked everything on association with the West. Even if five-year plans are a feature of the country's economic policy, these have nothing in the least to do with African socialism. The latter is a topic that tends to be discussed only half-heartedly.

**Agriculture** remains the basis of the Kenyan economy as it always has been. Even though it accounts for only one third of the national income, it provides a living for more than 80% of the population, many of whom, nomads and small farmers in particular, farm in order to feed themselves.

Of major economic importance are the crops grown for export: coffee, tea, pyrethrum (the flowers of which are used to manufacture non-toxic insecticides), pineapple for canning, fresh flowers and vegetables (green beans, artichokes, avocados), and fruit (mangoes, papayas, passion-fruit). These bring much-needed foreign revenue into the country.

In a joint venture with the European Community, Kenya is at present vigorously promoting cultivation of that African staple, maize. By the end of the century, the country is expected to be a highly productive exporter, capable of providing for the less fortunate drought-ridden African states.

**Kenya has mineral resources**, at least in theory. Metals and precious stones have been found, but in such small quantities that they are not worth extracting. Only soda ash and fluorite have proved profitable. The Americans are prospecting for oil in the north of the country, with a good chance of success.

**Industry** in Kenya had shown a remarkable rate of growth until the start of the oil crisis. Then the shortage of foreign currency put an end to the boom. Rigorous import restrictions have drastically reduced the supply of foreign-branded articles, while at the same time difficulties in obtaining replacement parts have crippled many industrial enterprises. Punitive levies on imports (up to 200%) safeguard home industries (textiles, shoes, tyres) from foreign competition.

Even today a large number of businesses are controlled by foreign capital and operate under foreign management. This is not likely to change significantly in the near future, although the country aims eventually to Kenyanise its industry and restrict work permits for foreigners to those with irreplaceable skills.

**Tourism**, Kenya's second biggest earner of foreign currency, brings more than half a million visitors to the country every year. Most recently the government has been pursuing an ambitious plan to encourage a million foreign tourists to visit the country annually, looking especially to Japan, India and the Oil States.

## Many peoples, many tongues

Diversity is the order of the day in Kenya, especially as regards the population. To have more than forty peoples with more than forty languages – some related to each other, many utterly unalike – is something of a mixed blessing for a young state.

*Samburu warriors*

Many tribes live side by side to their mutual advantage; others by contrast have been hostile for centuries. Nomads are contemptuous of labouring in fields. Farmers despise nomads as primitives lagging behind the times. The people of the coast look down on both.

Following Kenyatta's death, the government made increasing efforts to bring about equality between the tribes. The motto under President Moi has become 'I no longer know tribes, I know only Kenyans', and it has been made illegal for the authorities to require people to declare from which tribe they come. No one who knows the strength of tribal identification will, however, be surprised to learn that tribal problems are still far from being resolved.

Kenya's population is now about 20 million, half of whom are under 15 years of age. The annual growth rate of 3.9% remains the highest in the world. Life expectancy is about 53 years.

Averaging 31 inhabitants per sq km, Kenya is much less densely populated than the UK, for example. Yet some rural areas, mainly around Lake Victoria, are hugely overpopulated, with 410 persons per sq km.

The proportion of non-Africans (some 30,000 Europeans, 80,000 Indians and 25,000 Arabs) is small, despite appearances to the contrary in the capital.

There can be few places in the world where such a colourful mix of races and cultures can be seen as in Nairobi: Africans of every sort, gaily fashionable or quietly British in dress, some in the traditional garb of the West Coast, others in the wretched rags of the slums; whites from all over the world, from shabby drop-outs to long-established settlers; Hindu women in brilliant saris; Sikhs with beards and turbans; Muslim women in black *bui-buis*; here and there Somalis in long airy robes; Ethiopian women in their white, vividly embroidered national dress....

Kenya attracts many peoples and many races, but it still cannot be said to be a melting pot. That idea of the fifties of a multiracial society has been only partially realised: people here live *side by side* but not *together*. Now as before different cultures keep themselves to themselves. You will sometimes find a mixed gathering at a party, but it will most likely be an official function of some sort. Mixed marriages are still rare.

Still, the degree of tolerance taken for granted in Kenya can only be dreamed about in most other countries.

## Bantu and Nilotics

Wherever the subject is the population of East Africa, sooner or later the terms *Bantu* and *Nilotics* will be used, often mistakenly with reference to racial origin. In fact each refers to those who speak any one of a particular family of languages. As far as it is now possible to tell, the Nilotic peoples arrived in East Africa about 2,000 years ago, the Bantu from the 12th c. onwards. The Bantu are thought to have come from somewhere in central Africa, perhaps from around the province of Shaba in present-day Zaïre. They now account for about two-thirds of the Kenyan population. The remaining third (including, for example, the Luo, Masai and Kalenjin) belong to the Nilotic peoples who migrated from what is now southern Sudan. Of the formerly dominant Cushitic-speaking peoples, only minorities (Galla, Somalis, Rendille) still live in Kenya. It is less useful to divide the Kenyan people according to their languages, however, than by their lifestyles as nomads, farmers or coast-dwellers.

## The nomads

From an outside observer's point of view, the nomads are the most 'exotic' of all Kenyans. The Masai – or Maasai, 'those who speak the Maa language' – are especially well known to Europeans. At first belittled by the British as savages fearful of water, they were later portrayed as a noble people, tall and slender, reckless of danger and defiant of death. It was even held that they were descendants of the Roman legionnaires, presumably because of their sometimes classical features and the toga-like way they wear their wraps.

What can be said with certainty is that the Masai came from the north – possibly from Ethiopia – in the middle of the present millenium, and that during the last century they dominated large areas of East Africa. Epidemics and tribal feuding then weakened them irreversibly. The final blow was dealt by the British, who hounded them from their fertile grazing lands in the highlands into the dry regions of the Sudan. Today about 220,000 Masai are still found in Kenya. Those who pursue their traditional way of life face increasing difficulties in today's Kenya.

Traditionally the Masai lived exclusively from their cattle. The number of cows, not their quality, determined the status of a man and his family. Cattle were therefore considered too valuable to eat and were only slaughtered on ceremonial occasions. Goats and sheep provided meat, and asses transport. It is only recently that maize-meal and tea have become accepted as foods alongside meat, milk and blood.

More and more Masai are now coming to realise that neither they nor their land can sustain large herds of inferior quality animals. They are improving their stock and raising cattle with the efficiency of ranchers. Nor do they any longer have scruples about putting a value on a cow in Kenyan shillings.

Most Masai nowadays have permanent homes, frequently the traditional *man-yattas* of clay and cow-dung but increasingly a square-shaped house made of wood or corrugated iron. They and their cattle will now only move long distances in times of drought. As a result, greater numbers of their children have the opportunity to go to school, where they not only learn to read and write but encounter new values and new ideas.

Since some families have begun to drop the practice of sending their sons to live as warriors, the traditional structure of the tribe is changing. Formerly the basis of every male Masai's life was membership of an age-set: child, warrior, elder, each with several subdivisions. As he reached each successive stage, his standing was enhanced. A male child enjoyed the greatest possible freedom, though he was expected to undertake some herding duties. Between the ages of 14 and 18, after many years of preparation and following ceremonial circumcision, he became a warrior. The warriors lived apart from the rest of the tribe but together with the girls of their age-group. Their responsibilities were then to protect the cattle from being preyed on by both humans and wild animals, and to enlarge the herd if possible by raiding. The Masai believe that when God created the world the Masai were given charge of all the cattle, and so it cannot be right if other tribes now own them too. Since their neighbours have very similar ideas, the round of cattle-thieving is unending. Rustling is primarily a way of meeting the often exorbitant demands of bride-money. At about the age of thirty the pleasant warrior-days came to an end. The Masai cut off his elaborate hair-do, married and became an elder whose advice everyone was supposed to respect.

The signs that a society which has managed to survive relatively unscathed is now beginning to crumble can be seen particularly in Nairobi. Young warriors, many dressed in all their finery, hire themselves out for a pittance as night-watchmen. During the day they wander like lost souls through the more wretched parts of the city, sometimes falling spontaneously into one of their traditional dances; or they stand in hairdressers' salons selling their hair, which they wear in the proud style of the Masai warrior, to fashionable city ladies. The Masai are having to pay a high price for their wish to retain their traditional way of life. Few seem likely to make such a successful leap into the new society as George Saitoti – Kenya's finance minister.

The Samburu, Rendille, Pokot, Gabbra and Boran also belong to the nomadic peoples.

## The farmers

Totalling almost four million, the Kikuyu are the biggest tribe in Kenya. Their homeland, which they left 600 years ago for the East African highlands, was in what is now Somalia.

According to Kikuyu legend, their tribal ancestors *Gikuyu* and *Mumbi* were taken by God to the slopes of Mount Kenya and given all the land that lay stretched out at their feet. He also presented them with nine daughters, whose names the branches of the tribe bear to this day. Even after God had given the nine daughters nine husbands, the women continued to have the say among the Kikuyu, a situation that changed only when the Kikuyu adopted the social structures of the Masai, whom they displaced. Recognising the advantages of having a warrior-group of their own, they too came to divide their lives into age-sets of child, warrior and elder.

Links between the Masai and the Kikuyu have always been close, even to the extent of intermarriage. The Masai valued their Kikuyu neighbours particularly for their skill as makers of weapons. Jomo Kenyatta, in his book *Facing Mount Kenya*, tells the story of how the Kikuyu came to use iron: In the beginning God shared all the animals out among both the men and the women. Since meat was needed for the table, the women started to slaughter their animals. But they only had wooden knives, and the animals soon became tired of the wretched jabbing. They fled to freedom and became wild. Fearful of losing their animals too, the men went back to God, who then had an inspiration. He made them a gift of iron, which the animals apparently considered an improvement. In any case they stayed.

The Kikuyu are not only great story-tellers, they are also adaptable and open – perhaps too open – to new ideas. In the colonial period it was they who chiefly suffered, since they occupied the most fertile and hence the most sought-after land. During the Mau Mau revolt they also bore the brunt of the fatalities. It was the Kikuyu, on the other hand, who best understood European ways of doing things, ways which they had no inhibitions about following. They came, therefore, to occupy the leading positions in independent Kenya and extended their power at the expense of other tribes. In doing so they have lost much of their tradition and their identity. No other people in East Africa has changed quite as much as the Kikuyu.

Today the Kikuyu share the serious problems posed by a shortage of land with the other farming peoples, the Luo and Luya (tribes of 2.5 million each) and the Kamba and Kalenjin (2 million each). Since they all practise division of inheritance, many find their fields too small to feed a family. Their only option then is to move to the misery of Nairobi, where opportunities for them are minimal.

For these people a piece of land is the most precious thing on earth, and even those who now live in the towns will go to any lengths to acquire a little plot somewhere, a *shamba*. While this deep-seated love of land is something that unites the farming tribes, it can also act as a touch-paper when it comes to disputes over land.

## The peoples of the coast

The coastal tribes are numerically small and their social structure is less easily defined. In addition to being farmers and fishermen, they are also merchants and artisans.

Of the nine tribes – Giriama, Kauma, Chonyl, Jibana, Kamba, Ribe, Rubai, Duruman and Digo – the Giriama are the best known. It is almost certainly the Giriama you will encounter at any folk evening in a beach hotel. They, unlike their neighbours, have remained relatively untouched by Islam, and being considered more African in consequence have greater appeal for tourism. The tribe now supports itself almost entirely from foreign tourists. The Giriama act out 'traditional tribal life' in ethnic villages, putting their hearts into 'traditional dances' which, whatever else they may be, are certainly not traditional. Dance as a performance is a wholly un-African notion. Anyone mistaken enough to judge the very real Giriama gift for music and dance from their folk performances would be doing them a grave injustice.

Essentially, all the coastal tribes are orientated more towards the sea, and to India and Arabia, than they are to their own hinterland. Islam has been established here for centuries. Even if the religion is not enforced with full Arab rigour – and even if the girls use their *bui-buis* (similar to the *chadors* worn in Iran) as much to flirt behind as

*Left: Masai girls; top right: Giriama dancers; bottom right: students in Nairobi*

to conceal themselves – it would be dangerous to underestimate the underlying seriousness with which Islamic principles are held. The people of the coast have perhaps become accustomed to the idea that many Europeans enjoy unrestricted freedom, but they are far from approving of it. The ban on nude and topless bathing, for example, should certainly not be ignored. Nevertheless, there is clearly a considerable amount of prostitution in the port of Mombasa.

## The Indians

That there is an Indian population to be mentioned at all is entirely the responsibility of the British, who brought Indians to Kenya from the subcontinent to build the Uganda railway. Despite having endured often inhumane conditions, when their contracts were completed the Indians did not want to leave. Like the British, they saw an opportunity to get a toe-hold for themselves in this new country. Kenya was their America. Banned from acquiring land in the 'white man's country', they were forced to set up in trade, and despite African attempts to take over they still control 90% of the country's small businesses. Not surprisingly this arouses strong feelings, especially because the Indians tend to resist integration into an African Kenya.

The Indian presence in Kenya gives visitors the added bonus of experiencing a little bit of Asia – Indian art, Indian cinema, Indian food and Indian music all flourish. Of course there is also diversity within the Indian community, with three religious groups predominating.

The **Hindus** are, if anything, more conservative than their counterparts in India. Almost without exception the women wear saris – 5.5 m of material skilfully draped around the body. Male dominance within the family hierarchy is overwhelming. Among Hindus there is great disparity in social conditions.

The **Sikhs**, whose religion incorporates ideas drawn from both Hinduism and Islam, have mainly established themselves as artisans and builders. Adult men wear turbans and beards, and share a common surname, Singh, which means 'lion'.

The **Ismailites** wield the greatest economic influence (banks, insurance companies) and are very public-spirited (the quite exceptional Ismaili schools and hospitals are open to everyone). Their religious leader is the Aga Khan, who, on any official business in Kenya, is treated like a head of state. Anyone who spends a night at a *Serena Hotel* can enjoy the thought of the Aga Khan being one of the proprietors.

In a country with forty peoples and forty languages, things can only run smoothly if everyone is at least bi- or even better trilingual. Although Kenya's schools are as yet nowhere near to accomplishing this task, you will find no shortage of travelling companions with a fluent command of English, Swahili and their own mother tongue.

## The Kenyan way of life

Few visitors really appreciate how radical has been the social revolution forced upon Kenya, as indeed upon most of the African countries, in recent years. We tend to be struck only by the problems: the rural population fails to keep pace with economic development, falling ever further behind; the gap between the rich and the poor widens.

Every African child used to be brought up to a secure place in a tight-knit community. Each tribe would instil into its youngsters how vulnerable any individual was, how survival lay rather in communal life. Children would not be reared by their parents, but all together in their age-group, and in some tribes were even 'exchanged' within the extended family. Ensuring collective survival left little place for personal ambition.

The conversion of Africans to Western-style individualism has had devastating consequences. Self-interest, hitherto suppressed by years of tribal upbringing, is nowadays no longer restrained. Africans too are after a quick buck. And many who achieve success seem to care little for those who will never have the same chance. The country's motto remains '*Harambee*' – 'Together we will succeed.' But where is this togetherness to be found today?

In Kenya there is a free health service, but there are too few doctors, and

Kikuyu settlement

Local bus, Nairobi

medicines are in desperately short supply. There is free primary education, but too few schools and almost no books. Pensions are virtually unheard of outside the civil service. And although there is a legal minimum wage, employers who fail to pay it escape punishment. People who lose their jobs receive no welfare benefits, ending up as likely as not in trouble with the police. They become a burden on a family that is no longer equipped to offer the social and economic security of pre-colonial times.

## Bride-money

Some of the old customs survive, despite having lost their social relevance. Many Kenyans defend them nevertheless, determined to preserve whatever remains that is *African*. The result is seldom more than a meaningless caricature of the original.

Bride-money was not, as Europeans often seem to think, payment for the purchase of a wife. It was actually the African way of providing for the young married couple. The amount of bride-money was set by the tribal elders and reflected the

Brightly painted eating-place

Fetching the milk, Isiolo

status of the bride's family. In part it compensated the bride's parents for the loss of her labour and in part gave the woman herself a certain economic independence – if her marriage were to fail, she could go back to her parents and live from her bride-money (paid as a rule in cattle). At the same time, the payment represented a commitment by the husband to his new wife's family.

In rural areas the system still functions to some extent. But among urban dwellers bride-money is often demanded by parents simply for the sake of the transaction (and is paid in cash). There are newspaper reports of parents taking fourteen-year-old girls out of school and 'selling' them to aged husbands. Several such marriages have been legally annulled and the children returned to school. In a letter to the editor of the *Daily Nation*, one despairing young man called for the government to fix the price of a bride just as it does for maize and sugar.

## Circumcision

Ceremonial circumcision used to be the consummation of a long period of tribal preparation. By submitting to the pain, young men proved themselves worthy of full tribal membership.

Circumcision was thus more a social practice than a medical procedure. Anyone who remained uncircumcised was denied full tribal rights and could not marry. But equally they could not be pursued for an offence, being considered little different from an underage child. It was practices such as circumcision that led missionaries in particular to denounce Africans for their barbaric customs, completely overlooking the social significance. The Kikuyu, torn between their African heritage and European education, send their sons to hospital for the operation. It is no longer part of a process of tribal upbringing. There will, in any case, soon be no more tribal elders left to pass on the purely oral traditions. Female circumcision was once widely practised but is now illegal.

## Polygamy

Many Kenyans are polygamous. The Koran, as is well known, permits Muslims up to four wives. Traditional African religions allow any number, and Christians in Kenya – committed Catholics apart – are not always strictly monogamous either. Economic circumstances and the wife's level of education tend to be the decisive factors. Urban Kenyans, for instance, find several wives no longer affordable. For them polygamy is scarcely practicable financially, and psychologically speaking not possible at all.

For a Luo farmer living on the land, however, the situation is quite different. To him a wife is another pair of hands, so the more wives he has, the larger his undertaking can be. Rural women see things in very much the same light. Marriage here has almost nothing to do with love and romance and everything to do with status and security.

Europeans tend to have somewhat imaginative ideas about the sexual behaviour of Africans. In reality Kenyans are considerably more strait-laced than Europeans are ready to believe. A broken marriage is a serious matter, and the growing number of illegitimate children results from the young no longer receiving a traditional tribal education and lacking the protection of the community. Sheer necessity often drives young girls to prostitution.

## Rich and poor

Need is a very real factor in the lives of many Kenyans. Whilst a small, super-rich upper class (mainly Kikuyu) flies to London to shop and sends its children to exclusive universities in England and the USA, the vast majority of Kenyans struggle for the basics of daily life. Economic advancement is difficult, even impossible, when the unpredictable forces of nature can destroy everything you have struggled for, when there is no market for your produce and no means of transport, and when you lack education or the opportunity to use it.

# A wealth of religions

If there is one thing Kenyans find difficult to understand, it is that there are people with no belief in God. They themselves are profoundly religious. The diversity of landscape, peoples and languages is as nothing in comparison with the vast number of religions that exist together in Kenya. Only in summary are things simple: 50% of Kenyans are Christian; 10% Muslim; the rest belong to various Indian religions or to traditional African ones.

The Christians, of whom there are more than nine million, belong to eight hundred different churches (yes, *eight hundred*). The seeds of disunity that missionaries have brought to the country ever since the mid-19th c. have evidently sprouted here. Since religious freedom is guaranteed, anyone who feels the calling can establish his own church. And many do. They attract worshippers who are alienated by the official churches' lack of understanding of African traditions and ideas.

Such schism is not confined to Kenya's Christians. The Hindus are similarly divided, this time into fifty different groups, and Muslims too show a surprising diversity. Generally speaking the farming tribes (Kikuyu, Luo, Luya, Kamba) are Christian; the coastal peoples are Muslim; and the nomads follow traditional African religions. (It is only since 1960 that missionaries have been allowed among the Turkana.)

There are, of course, differences between the traditional African religions too. Common to all, however, is belief in God. He usually lives far away and does not concern himself with people. He does not want to be specially venerated but when people are in need they can turn to him and can count on his help. Also universal is a belief in ancestors who live on in a different form after death and continue to participate in the fate of both family and tribe. The ancestors behave just as moodily and unpredictably as living people. It is important therefore not to cross them and to appease them as a precautionary measure with offerings of food. The ancestors only really die when the family line itself dies out and there is no one left to think of them. This is one of the basic reasons for the large number of children in Kenya. After their final demise, the ancestors turn into spirits, becoming impersonal and sometimes also god-like.

The task of mediating between humans, on the one hand, and God, spirits and the ancestors, on the other, falls to the medicine man. Unlike that of African magicians and witches, his role is a beneficial one. Africans believe that bad luck and illness are the result of wrongdoing. So a medicine man's first step is to enquire into any such cause. While the rites that this involves once brought him into disrepute with Europeans, it is generally acknowledged nowadays that illness often has social origins. What was once mocked as African quackery has today been largely accepted. Contemporary African medicine is glad to draw on the wisdom of the medicine man and in some modern Kenyan clinics his advice is deliberately sought. Generally speaking, medicine in Africa advances by combining traditional learning with modern knowledge.

## Art and literature

Anyone in search of abbeys, cathedrals, tapestries and paintings will inevitably conclude that there is no trace of culture in Kenya. The nomads have built no magnificent houses and erected no monumental cult sites. The farmers have had no kings who thought it necessary to demonstrate their power by constructing impressive buildings. For the same reason art in East Africa has never been professionalised. Our concept of 'the artist' is completely unknown. Art for its own sake has up to now been quite foreign to Kenya.

There was always African art, however, in the work of its craftsmen. Those with the talent to carve well decorated the three-legged stools, the spoons and the bowls. Even the carved fetishes were never pure works of art, but ritual objects for everyday use. Because the materials with which these craftsmen worked were often perishable, few artefacts survive to demonstrate what artistry could be embodied in a calabash, or how elaborate a bead-covered leather dress could be. A century of colonialism has much to answer for, as African skills were first derided and then allowed to become forgotten.

Today some effort is being made to revive the ancient crafts. The results are, of course, no longer purely traditional, generally making concessions to European taste. Even so they are often very attractive.

Frequently overlooked is the fact that literature too is art. A visit to a Nairobi or Mombasa bookshop is always rewarding. If in particular you have driven through the rural countryside, or have witnessed the seedier side of Nairobi, you will appreciate the books by Ngugi wa Thiong'o or Meja Mwangi. They offer an authentic picture of a Kenya you cannot really expect to discover just on a holiday visit.

You can also find some exceptionally well-produced volumes of photographs on sale in Kenya.

**Swahili and Kiswahili:** The name 'Swahili' derives from the Arabic for 'coast-dweller' and refers to those who people the coast from the Horn of Africa to Mozambique. The prefix *ki* means 'language', so *Kiswahili* is the language of the

*Masai mask, spears and shield*

Swahili, a mixture of Arabic and Bantu with a dash of Portuguese. It spread into the interior with the trading caravans. Today Kiswahili is spoken in Kenya, Tanzania, northern Mozambique, in parts of Zaïre and Ruanda, and increasingly also in Uganda. But Swahili culture remains confined to the coast and in particular to the island of Lamu (see page 50) and Zanzibar.

See 'Useful words and phrases', page 89.

# Shopping

Whatever you buy in Kenya, you can be sure it has been produced specially for tourists. 'Authentic' Kenyan souvenirs are virtually impossible to find.

**Kangas** are among the most popular buys. They are lengths of imaginatively decorated printed cotton and are usually worn wound round the hips. Look around the beach and you will see kangas being worn in an unbelievable variety of ways.

**Kikois** are the lengths of striped cotton sported by men on the coast. With stripes in every imaginable colour, there is almost no limit to their use — as clothing, turban, bath-towel or table-cloth.

**Kikapus** are equally practical and are one of the few products not manufactured only for the souvenir market. They are hard-wearing bags, woven from sisal, usually with leather straps. They are made by the Kamba and Kikuyu in the Kenyan interior.

**Jewellery** of every sort is available. Prettiest of all are metal and leather chains, and strings of beads that make good costume jewellery. Although influenced by African tradition, the designers are often Europeans who have made Kenya their second home.

**Carvings** are unquestionably the most profitable commodity for the Kenyan souvenir industry. Whether any particular piece is or isn't a work of art can be debated, but all are hand-carved and usually of good quality. The choice ranges from toothpicks to life-size figures of Masai. The Kamba are Kenya's most gifted wood-carvers and it is after them that the Kamba figures are named. Also widely admired are the strange and rather attractive carvings of the Makonde. They are from Tanzania and northern Mozambique though, not Kenya.

**Ivory and animal skins** used to be the classic souvenirs from Kenya. Today trade in both is prohibited. Anything you are offered will almost certainly have been smuggled in from Tanzania or poached in Kenya and you will be well advised to refuse. Otherwise you risk being charged not only by the Kenyan police but also by your own Customs on your return home.

**Gemstones and semi-precious stones** such as amethyst, aquamarine, ruby, sapphire and rose quartz, as well as petrified wood and much else besides, are all found in Kenya. They are usually offered in simple settings. If you are likely to be interested, enquire about prices at home before you go — things are not necessarily cheaper in Kenya.

*Masai bead necklace*

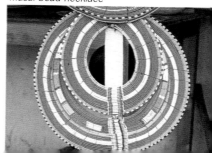

Among other souvenirs to be recommended are soapstone animals, batiks, baskets, sisal and banana-leaf matting, and many kinds of beadwork. The patchwork, produced mainly by women's groups in the urban slums, is highly unusual.

#  Food and drink

A country that counts its blessings when its people have enough to sustain life will rarely evolve a refined cuisine, especially when there has been no upper class to enjoy 'cultivation' at the expense of the poor.

Traditional Kenyan dishes are thus as simple as can be and seldom suited to tourists' stomachs. Even less likely to appeal is the nomad diet of milk, blood and fish (baked and without seasoning).

*Ugali,* a thick porridge made from white maize-meal (from millet as well in some parts) is the staple Kenyan meal. It is served with *sukuma* when available, a vegetable not unlike green kale. In the west of Kenya, people eat *matoke,* a pulp made from cooked bananas. The national dish of the Kikuyu is *irio* (see recipe). In country areas a beer as cloudy as it is intoxicating is brewed from maize or honey for special occasions.

---

Just in case you have a fancy for Kenyan food when you get home again, here are two recipes, each for four people.

### Irio

*Ingredients:* 4 large fresh corn cobs, 400 g pulses (as many varieties as possible) soaked overnight, 4 potatoes, 450 g spinach, salt and pepper.

Remove the corn from the cob and cook it in boiling water with the drained pulses until both are soft. Add the potatoes, peeled and cut into cubes. When they are almost cooked, drain and mix in the chopped spinach. When cooked, season with salt and pepper and mash together.

### Curried meat with spinach

*Ingredients:* 750 g spinach, 4 tbsp. oil, 1 tsp. sugar, 750 g boned leg of lamb, cut into 2 cm cubes, ¼ litre milk, ½ tsp. chilli powder, 2 tsp. ground coriander, 1 tsp. turmeric, 1 tsp. garam masala, salt.

Wash the spinach and remove the hard stems before cooking the leaves (without extra water) until soft. Strain off the fluid, putting it to one side, and make a purée of the cooked spinach. Heat the oil in a pan and mix in the sugar. After two minutes add the lamb and brown thoroughly, stirring continuously. Add the milk, salt, chilli and coriander, then leave to cook uncovered until the lamb is almost dry. Put in the spinach and stir again until all the liquid has evaporated. Sprinkle on the turmeric, pour on the spinach water, and continue cooking until the meat is tender, if necessary adding more water. When all the liquid has evaporated, mix in the garam marsala. Serve with bread or rice.

---

There is no need for tourists to despair about the food, however. Many of the hotels can be proud of their cuisine; Kenyan beef is excellent, and fresh fruit and vegetables are available the whole year round. The majority of tourist hotels offer international fare, more European than African – a breakfast buffet with juices, tropical fruit, cereal and eggs; at lunchtime a buffet with a large choice of salads and cold and hot dishes; an evening menu usually of five courses. Unfortunately it is only occasionally that any of the seafood with which the Indian Ocean teems – giant *crab*, *lobster* or *crayfish*, and *prawns* of every size – makes its appearance on the plate.

On the special 'Swahili evenings' fish is served, with coconut milk, *cassava* (a root similar to a potato) and coffee flavoured with ginger.

You will also be able to try the dishes the Kenyans have adopted from abroad, especially from Indian cuisine.

Freshly roasted corn on the cob makes a nice snack between meals and can be found on almost every street corner. There are banana chips and arrowroot crisps for nibbling, while for those who like something hotter there are Indian mixes with a wide variety of ingredients.

## Alcoholic and non-alcoholic drinks

Wine lists are nowhere very comprehensive. There is usually a selection of Italian and French wines, but they are very highly priced and have rarely been improved by being transported to Africa. There are also wines marked 'made in Kenya', mostly made from papayas. The first small Kenyan vintage of wine produced from grapes took place in 1985. The white wine from Lake Naivasha is excellent.

Otherwise people keep to the very pleasant beer that Kenya produces in abundance (for export too). Africans – Muslims apart – are committed beer-drinkers. But they prefer their beer warm, so it is as well when ordering to say if you want it cold.

Alcohol-free drinks include the sodas and lemonades well known to Europeans, and also fresh fruit-juices. The home-made passion-fruit juice can be highly recommended.

It comes as no surprise that Kenya takes great pride in its *coffee* and *tea*. A cup is always included in the price of any meal. In addition the good old British habit of *early morning tea* survives. In almost any hotel in the Kenyan interior you can arrange the evening before to be roused at a particular time next morning with a cup of tea.

*Western and local food available in Kenyan hotels*

*Gerenuk on Samburu Game Reserve*

## National parks and reserves

The trade in ivory and skins and the passion of European high society for big-game hunting had already decimated the country's wildlife within a few years of Kenya's being 'discovered'. As early as 1900 the plain by the River Athi became the first game reserve in East Africa – now the *Nairobi National Park*. Even before the First World War other reserves had been created. Independent Kenya adopted and expanded the conservation policy of the colonial era. The game parks and reserves are far from being simply a major investment for the benefit of tourism, however. Indeed, tourism passes by most of the thirty parks that now exist. They are an ecological success story that requires above all sacrifice on the part of the local population. Elephants, lions and baboons do not, after all, stop at park boundaries; they devastate surrounding fields and attack domestic herds. It is easy enough to preach sermons about 'animal conservation' from the comfortable distance of Europe; but in Africa, where a country may not know how its people are going to be fed, it would not be at all surprising if the priorities appeared very different.

In *national parks* conservation covers everything – landscape, animals and plants.

In *game reserves* and *national reserves* only the animals are protected and other activities continue within the reserve. So among the zebra, giraffe and wildebeest the Masai will be found grazing their cattle. Purists may turn up their noses, but it is precisely this sort of juxtaposition that allows a glimpse of Kenya as it was before Europeans arrived.

In parks and reserves make sure you do not leave your car under any circumstances. The contented-looking lion stretching lazily in the sun is not the well-behaved animal of the television series, and buffalo, especially solitary buffalo, are the most aggressive of all African animals. Even if you have your own transport, you should still hire the services of a ranger on entering the reserve, or at one of the lodges. He will know the places most frequented by wildlife. Many camps also organise safaris on foot. It is exciting to encounter the animals at their own level so to speak, but it is not without an element of risk.

Generally speaking all the safari locations are easily accessible from Mombasa or Nairobi. The 500 km that separate them cause few problems, the flight taking between fifty and ninety minutes depending on the type of plane. As a rule the parks are open throughout the year, though they can become impassable during the rainy season.

Entrance fees in Kenya are moderate compared with other African countries but they vary from park to park.

## National parks

**Aberdare National Park** (766 sq km) extends up to a height of about 4,000 m above sea-level. It has fascinating mountain scenery with magnificent vegetation, including bamboo forests, tree heaths and giant lobelias. Elephant, buffalo and leopard etc. inhabit the rain forest that covers the slopes, also — rather rare — the very shy bongo antelope.

**Amboseli National Park** (380 sq km) is the most photogenic of all the parks, having Mount Kilimanjaro for a backdrop. In the dry season it can boast one of the largest concentrations of animals in Africa.

**East Turkana National Park**, also known as Sibiloi Park (1,570 sq km), is the most remote park in Kenya and the least rich in wildlife. Chiefly it serves to protect the crocodiles in Lake Turkana. There are prehistoric excavation sites and petrified wood.

**Lake Nakuru National Park** (202 sq km) is a paradise for birds. Famous the world over, it is within easy reach of Nairobi, with flamingo colonies, pelican, heron and other waterfowl.

**Meru National Park** (820 sq km) is north-east of Mount Kenya and home of the (reintroduced) white rhino.

**Mount Elgon National Park** (160 sq km) is for the initiated who already know Kenya well. A 4,280-m-high volcanic massif on the Ugandan border, its slopes are covered with dense rain forest abounding in game. Elephant, buffalo and leopard congregate here. Caves, some up to 14 km in length, cut deep into the mountain-side.

**Mount Kenya National Park** (584 sq km) is the highest of all above sea-level, with Afro-alpine vegetation, elephant, buffalo and mountain leopard. Hill walking and climbing: *Batian* (5,199 m) and *Nelion* (5,188 m) are only for experienced mountaineers; *Lenana* (4,995 m) can be tackled by anyone who is fit.

**Nairobi National Park** (114 sq km) borders directly on to the capital's airport. Here almost all the 'important' animals, except elephant, can be seen on Nairobi's doorstep.

**Tsavo National Park** (20,000 sq km!), the country's largest park, is situated half-way between Nairobi and Mombasa. It is famous for its red elephants (tinged with the colour of the red laterite soil).

## Game reserves

**Lake Bogoria** (107 sq km) is a small park around a soda lake, with hot springs and flamingo colonies.

**Marsabit Game Reserve** (2,000 sq km), a forested reserve amidst the semi-desert of northern Kenya, has volcanic plugs, crater lakes and elephant with unusually large tusks.

**Masai Mara** (1,700 sq km) on the Tanzanian border has the greatest abundance of game. It forms a single ecological unit with the *Serengeti*. It has extensive hill scenery and is particularly impressive at the time of the wildebeest migration (the beginning of August).

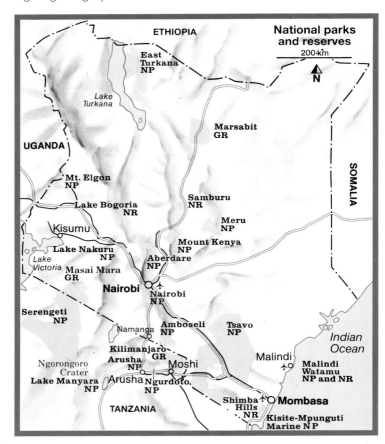

Baobab tree

Ostrich, Samburu

**Shimba Hills National Reserve** (192 sq km), right by the coast, is an area of exceptional scenic charm, with buffalo, roan and sable antelope, and birds.

**Samburu** (225 sq km) is on the threshold of the dry north of Kenya. All the usual animals are to be found in reserves on either side of the Uaso Nyiro River; in addition, there are reticulated giraffe, Grevy's zebra and gerenuk (or Walter's gazelle).

**Shaba Game Reserve** is a small reserve north-east of Samburu.

Two areas in the Indian Ocean have been designated underwater reserves:

**Malindi and Watamu National Park and Reserve** (15 sq km): coral, sea shells and fish; snorkelling and 'safaris' in glass-bottomed boats.

**Kisite-Mpunguti Marine National Park** (25 sq km) consists of four coral islands some 70 km south of Mombasa. Snorkelling expeditions are arranged.

---

### Vast numbers, many kinds

An aerial census conducted not long ago by KREMU, a department of the Kenyan Ministry of the Environment, recorded:

| | | | |
|---|---|---|---|
| Elephant | 39,000 | Wildebeest | 1,263,000 |
| Buffalo | 73,000 | Gerenuk | 54,000 |
| Rhinoceros | 500 | Waterbuck | 28,000 |
| Giraffe | 79,000 | Ostrich | 36,000 |
| Zebra | 230,000 | Warthog | 26,000 |
| Grant's gazelle | 307,000 | Eland | 35,000 |
| Thomson's gazelle | 83,000 | Lion: no data – they are too difficult |
| Impala | 104,000 | to spot from the air. |

△ Rock hyrax

Elephant ▷

Rhinoceros △

◁ Cape buffalo

Hippopotamus ▽

# The wildlife of East Africa

The following is only a selection, and the details are unavoidably abbreviated. (Swahili names in brackets.)

**Elephant** *(tembo)*, the largest living land mammal. The African elephant can be up to 3.5 m in height and 4 m in length, weighing between 5,000 and 7,000 kg. Its tusks average 2.5 m and weigh 50 kg. It is distinguished from the Indian elephant by its larger ears and less rounded back. Elephants are social animals, mainly living in herds of varying sizes, though solitary bull elephants are not uncommon. Elephants are vegetarian and require large quantities of food. Their gestation period is 22 to 24 months and lifespan about 60 years — 80 years at most. Although generally of a peaceful disposition, they can be very dangerous if they or their young seem threatened.

**Rock hyrax** *(pimbi)* are similar in size and shape to a marmot but actually a close relative of the elephant! They live among boulders or in rocky terrain, and can also often be seen in the vicinity of lodges. Other species of hyrax are tree-dwelling.

**Rhinoceros** *(faru)* weigh between 1,000 and 2,000 kg. The front horn is between 50 and 100 cm long, the rear horn about 50 cm; the cows often have longer, thinner horns. Gestation period 17 to 18 months, one calf. Rhinos live in pairs or in small family groups, usually not straying far from the same area. They eat twigs, shoots, leaves and roots. They have a good sense of hearing and smell but poor sight. They may be very irritable, especially in the rutting season when the bulls may fight fiercely over the cows. It is sometimes claimed that rhinos that come galloping up snorting are not being aggressive but merely curious (being so short-sighted). You would be very ill-advised to put this personally to the test!

**Hippopotamus** *(kiboko)* grow to over 4 m in length and 1.5 m in height and weigh between 2,000 and 4,000 kg. Hippos live in rivers and lakes, preferring shallow water close to grassland on which they graze at night. During the day usually only their eyes and noses are to be seen protruding from the water. They are able to stay submerged for more than four minutes.

**Buffalo** *(nyati)* can weigh up to 800 kg. Their great horns, which have a span of between 100 and 300 cm, thicken out massively where they meet on the forehead. Buffalo often live in large herds and like to be near water. They drink regularly, eat grass, love wallowing and have a good sense of smell and hearing. Old bulls often leave the herd. Beware especially of solitary animals.

**Antelope and gazelle:** A simple rule of thumb (and it is no more than that) is: all gazelle are antelope, but some antelope are not gazelle. As a rough guide, these tend to be the larger, fast-running species, as opposed to the smaller, springing, gazelle.

**Gazelle:** The most common are the little *Thomson's gazelle (swala tomi)* and the larger *Grant's gazelle (swala granti)*. Thomson's gazelle are up to 70 cm at the shoulder, reddish sandy in colour, with a white underbelly and black stripes on the sides. Grant's gazelle, as much as 88 cm at the shoulder, are fawn with a white underbelly and rudimentary tail. Both sexes have horns. Thomson's and Grant's gazelle inhabit open savannah, grassland or scrub. They live in herds, usually of twenty to fifty animals but sometimes of several hundred.

**Impala** *(swala pala)*, are also a kind of gazelle. Anything up to 107 cm at the shoulder, they are reddish fawn with white underbelly and distinctive black stripes on their white hind legs. Only the bucks have the lyre-shaped horns.

**Gerenuk or Walter's gazelle** *(swala twiga)*, 90 to 105 cm at the shoulder, are slender and graceful with very long necks and long legs. Only the bucks have horns. Their favourite food is acacia leaves, which they reach by standing on their hind legs. They manage well with little water. In flight the body is carried low and the head and neck are thrust forward, allowing the animal to pass easily under the branches of the thorn bushes.

**Wildebeest** *(nyumbu)* are heavy, thickset antelope with a shoulder hump, mane on the neck and throat, and a horse-like tail. Their habitat is in open country and savannah; they live sometimes in very large herds and often in the company of zebra. The bulls are occasionally solitary.

**Waterbuck** *(kudu)*, large, powerful antelope 100 to 130 cm in height, with a thick, wiry coat and simple, curved horns, are always found in the vicinity of water, in damp forests and watery depressions. Two subspecies are found in Kenya: the *common waterbuck* (with the pale elliptical patch on its hindquarters) and *Defassa's waterbuck*.

**Eland** *(mbunju)*, 180 cm at the shoulder, are the largest antelope. Both sexes have thick, spiral horns. They live in small herds on the open plains as well as in the highlands and bush woodland. *Kongoni (kongoni)*, also known as Coke's hartebeest, are another species of large antelope. Growing to 122 cm at the shoulder, they have distinctive long,

narrow heads and sloping backs. Both sexes have short, powerful horns that curve out to the side. *Topi (nyamera)* are not unlike kongoni but darker and with blue-black fore and hind legs. The horns of both males and females bend upwards and backwards.

**Beisa oryx** *(choroa)*, 100 to 120 cm at the shoulder, weigh 180 to 225 kg. A grey to reddish-grey antelope, with white underbelly and sharply contrasting black and white facial markings. Both sexes have very long, straight, grooved horns, sometimes more than a metre in length.

**Bushbuck** *(mbawala)* are deer-like antelope, 65 cm (females) to 100 cm (bucks) at the shoulder, with distinctive white stripes running along the back as far as the flanks. They have the relatively high, powerful rump typical of forest antelope. Bucks have twisted horns, up to 55 cm in length, and darker body colouring.

**Kirk's dikdik** *(dikidiki)* is the smallest antelope (only 35 to 40 cm at the shoulder). It has tufts of hair on its head, and both sexes boast short, pointed horns. Usually living in pairs or in small family groups, it is found in dry open scrub, coastal scrubland or bush woodland.

**Giraffe** *(twiga)*, grow to 3.5 m at the shoulder. Males can sometimes be as tall as 6 m, though cows seldom exceed 4.8 m. Living alone or in herds of up to thirty or forty animals, they browse on the leaves and twigs of the acacia tree, and spread their long legs wide apart to drink. The horns on the forehead are covered with skin. They have a very characteristic way of galloping, as if in slow-motion. In East Africa there are three subspecies: the most common is the *Masai giraffe*, which has vine-leaf markings; less common (and seen

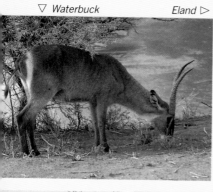
▽ Waterbuck

Eland ▷

△ Grant's gazelle

◁ Gerenuk
▽ Impala

△ Thomson's gazelle

▽ Beisa oryx

mostly in northern Kenya) is the *reticulated giraffe*, with white mesh-like markings; rarest of all is the *Uganda* or *Rothschild's giraffe*, again with mesh-like markings but this time in yellowy-brown and with well-formed horns on the forehead.

**Zebra** *(punda milia)* are of two kinds: the very widespread *common zebra*, thickset with broad stripes, and *Grevy's zebra*, lighter in build and with narrower stripes. The latter are mainly seen in northern Kenya. Zebra live in large herds on the dry open plains and in scrubland, often in company with wildebeest. Males fight one another standing side by side, head to tail, biting and kicking until one gives in.

**Warthog** *(ngiri)* stand 60 to 85 cm at the shoulder and like zebra are very widespread. They have a grey hide, almost completely without hair, a long bristly mane on the shoulders and neck, and large 'warts' on the side of the head in the area of their 40-cm-long tusks. They live in family groups, feeding on berries, roots and tubers. Their tails stand up vertically when they flee.

**Bush pig** *(nguruwe)* are 60 to 80 cm at the shoulder, light to dark brown with a white mane on the back and predominantly white head. Long, usually light-coloured tufts by the ears. Moving about in groups of anything from five to fifteen animals, they are rarely seen, being active mainly at night and during the twilight hours.

**Lion** *(simba)* are 2.5 to 3 m in length and about 1 m at the shoulder. The male has the familiar mane. The gestation period of 105 to 113 days generally produces three or four cubs. Lifespan: fifteen to twenty years. Lions live in family groups or prides of between five and twenty-five animals, each pride occupying a territory of its own. Lions hunt as a team (zebra, wildebeest, antelope, giraffe). A lion's roar is seldom a matter of the hunter giving voice; it is more often an audible marking out of the pride's territory. Lions inhabit sparse woodland, dry scrub, open plains and also rocky terrain. In the reserves they generally seem docile, even sleepy. But that should on no account mislead you into taking risks!

**Leopard** *(chui)*, about 70 cm at the shoulder, 2 to 3 m in length, weigh 60 to 75 kg. A gestation period of 92 to 95 days produces up to four cubs. Lifespan: fifteen to twenty years. Leopard live in forest, savannah, scrubland, semi-desert and rocky, mountainous terrain. They are very adaptable animals, living alone or in pairs, and hunting mainly at night (antelope, warthog, baboon). The kill is often hauled up into a tree where it will be safe from lions and hyenas.

**Cheetah** *(duma)* are long-legged and slender, with a noticeably small head and light golden-yellow coat with round black spots. Unlike other cats, adult cheetahs are unable to retract their claws. They live alone, in pairs or in family groups. They hunt by day, stalking their quarry (antelope, gazelle) and able to pursue them at great speed (90 to 100 kph) over short distances.

**Hyena** *(fisi)* are 60 to 80 cm at the shoulder. Of the two subspecies in Kenya, the *spotted hyena* is rarer than the *striped hyena*. Predominantly nocturnal but sometimes seen during the day, hyenas are scavengers and carrion-eaters, but also predators, hunting in packs (zebra and large antelope). The night howl of a hyena is very distinctive, like an eerie laugh.

△ Leopard
◁ Giraffe
▽ Crocodile

△ Black and white colobus
Black-faced vervet ◁
Jackal ▷

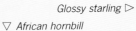
Glossy starling ▷
▽ African hornbill

△ Maribou stork    △ Sacred ibis

▽ African wood ibis  Crested crane ▷

**Jackal** *(mbweha)* are 40 to 45 cm at the shoulder. There are three types: the yellowy-brown or reddish-grey *golden jackal*, the grey-brown *side-striped jackal* with light stripes on its flanks, and, most commonly seen, the *black-backed jackal* with its black 'saddlecloth' flecked with silver. Mainly nocturnal, they roam in pairs across the open plains and scrub, feeding on both small animals and carrion.

**Anubis baboon** *(nyani)* are found in scrubland, savannah and rocky terrain. They live in groups of from twenty to over a hundred animals, within which a strict social hierarchy is observed. Baboons are by nature shy but can become very bold in the reserves if fed. Take great care not to be scratched or bitten.

**Black-faced vervet** *(tumbili)*, a monkey, grows to between 40 and 60 cm, with a tail 50 to 70 cm long. It has a black muzzle framed by a white beard and white band across the forehead. Vervet are at home both in trees and on the ground, living in groups of between twenty and thirty animals. Preferred habitat: acacia forest near rivers and lakes.

**Guereza or black and white colobus** *(mbega)*, another monkey, grows to between 60 and 75 cm, and is black with white side-whiskers and white tufts on body and tail. A forest-dweller, it is an agile climber and jumper, its coat fanning out like a parachute as it bounds through the trees. It lives in small groups and it eats leaves and shoots.

**Crocodile** *(mamba)* can be found in almost all the waters of tropical and subtropical Africa. Growing to 5 m and occasionally 6 or 7 m in length, crocodile often live to be over a hundred years old. They are extremely dangerous. Despite their somnolent appearance, they can move very quickly.

## Birds

There are almost twice as many species of bird in Kenya as are found in the whole of Europe – more than eight hundred different varieties, 10% of the world's total. This incredible richness makes Kenya particularly attractive to ornithologists and birdwatchers from all over the world. The birds, moreover, are quite easy to observe: seldom harried, they have no need to be wary.

The 'greatest bird show on earth' is found at Lake Nakuru. Several million red *lesser flamingo* congregate in the shallow waters, encircling the lake in a pinky red ribbon. They feed on the tiny, spiral-shaped algae that thrive in the salty water. Large numbers of *pelican* and various kinds of *heron, cormorant* and *kingfisher* also gather here. On the banks huge *maribou* storks can be seen (they also like to scavenge around the lodges in the national parks – like a gang of ecological dustmen).

Another variety of stork, the very distinctive *African wood ibis*, is most commonly seen on the flat banks of rivers and lakes. Here the black and white *sacred ibis* also pokes about for food with its long, curved bill. The *blacksmith plover*, another black and white bird, is found on grassland and near lodges.

On the big plains the *crested crane*, one of the loveliest of all the African bird species, struts about in pairs or little groups. The black *African hornbill* is highly unusual. Its diet consists mainly of snakes and small lizards. To be seen almost everywhere is the brightly tri-coloured *glossy starling*, which enjoys feasting off the bait put down at the animal feeding-places.

◁ *Pelican and flamingo on Lake Nakuru*

# Hints for your holiday

*Masai
warriors*

One or two points to help you avoid giving offence to your Kenyan hosts:
– keep your cool even if things do not always go smoothly. By losing your composure over trifles you will only make yourself look ridiculous in African eyes and forfeit respect.
– be sparing with criticism, and never be openly critical of another person.
– avoid public displays of affection. Physical contact between men and women in public is frowned upon, though Kenyan men think nothing of crossing the street holding hands. African body language is different and should not be interpreted by the 'rules' of other countries.
– wear beach clothes only on the beach.
– do not keep harping on about how efficient things are elsewhere. Nothing you do or say can alter the fact that Kenya operates on its own terms.
– ask permission before photographing anyone. Africans not unreasonably feel a distinction is in order between people and the animals in a reserve; their unease at being photographed should be respected.

There are also a number of dos and don'ts that will help you avoid becoming too closely acquainted with a Kenyan police station or even prison:
– always stand for the national anthem (at the beginning of theatre and cinema performances or television programmes as well as when the national flag is raised or lowered). Unfamiliarity is no excuse.
– never publicly criticise the President.
– do not abuse Kenyan banknotes, even in jest.
– resist offers of illegally traded ivory and skins and do not be tempted to take animal bones from the national parks as souvenirs. Shell-collecting is also forbidden (as, incidentally, is nude bathing).
– be careful about what you photograph. Taking photos of the military, the police, airports, the national flag, parliament or the President (except on officially approved occasions) is likely to land you in real trouble with the authorities.

# Where to go and what to see

## The coast

Most holidaymakers in Kenya arrive at Mombasa. First impressions can be something of a disappointment. The drive from Moi airport through the outskirts of Mombasa hardly suggests a holiday paradise. Nor, no matter how long and hard you look, will you see any sign of an ocean; not until after you have checked into your hotel will you catch any real sight of it.

According to the holiday statistics, though, only about half of those arriving will be taken by surprise; every second tourist will have been to Kenya before. What better recommendation could there be than this high number of returning holidaymakers — exceptionally high for a long-haul destination?

Up to now only part of the 400-km-long coast has been opened to tourism: about 20 km around Malindi and about 60 km either side of Mombasa. The beach is mainly flat with fine sand, but in places interspersed with sharp-edged coral outcrops. Along its whole length the coast is fringed by an almost continuous reef. This keeps the sharks away and subdues the sometimes mighty breakers. Except for river estuaries, the water is crystal-clear almost everywhere, frequently being the turquoise colour typical of the South Seas.

*The Indian Ocean*

## Holidaying by the sea

 **Some points to remember**

Swimming inside the coral reef at high water is ordinarily quite safe. But not even experienced swimmers should venture out beyond the reef on account of the strong currents and the danger of sharks. In most places the water lying between the beach and the reef drops to only knee-deep at low tide. You can then either resort to the hotel pool or take a walk out to the reef. Tough plastic sandals or at least plimsolls are essential.

*Glass-bottomed boats* are a feature of the coast. But you can get an even closer look at the corals, fish and starfish by snorkelling. Most hotels will hire out masks and flippers.

Sadly the variety of species on the reef has been greatly reduced in recent years by unrestrained shell-collectors — tourists as well as natives — plundering the seabed and trampling down coral colonies. Conservation measures taken by the government came too late and are not fully observed even today. So the real thrills of snorkelling can only be experienced nowadays at one or two places on the coast and in the marine parks and reserves.

Snorkelling is safe enough in theory, but you should avoid touching everything you see. Many creatures sting or bite, while others secrete poisons harmful to the skin. But the greatest danger when snorkelling is the equatorial sun. A T-shirt gives the best protection.

Windsurfers should already have had some experience before setting out if unsupervised. Hotels and watersports clubs offer instruction, and you can, of course, learn diving and sailing too.

Most importantly: do not let this blissful beach existence lull you into taking risks. If you venture out too far in a boat or on a surfboard, you cannot count on speedy help if you get into trouble. There are no lifeboats waiting to be called out.

Another thing people tend to forget is that the equatorial sun can literally burn holes in your skin, Overcast skies are particularly dangerous, and anyone who skimps on suntan oil (take it with you from home) will certainly regret it. Nor is it sensible to take valuables (money, jewellery, photographic equipment) to the beach; in a Third World country like Kenya it is asking for trouble to display wealth openly. Most thefts and muggings would be avoided if tourists took heed of the old maxim that 'opportunity makes the thief'.

You will receive reminders in your hotel that nude and topless bathing is forbidden.

For the more energetic among the landlubbers, tennis, golf and, in some places, squash are available.

Children are very well catered for on the Kenyan coast, though special precautions should be taken to see they are protected from the harmful effects of the sun overhead and the sea urchins and suchlike below (they can injure feet). This done, a walk over the sea bottom newly exposed by the tide can be a constant source of excitement and delight.

There is little at the coast apart from the beach hotels — no holiday resorts as such and few independent restaurants, nightclubs or discothèques. Social life is therefore centred on the hotels themselves, and their staff lay on programmes of dancing, folk evenings and other entertainment.

*Tusk arches, Mombasa*

# Mombasa Pop. 500,000

Mombasa is the second largest city in Kenya and the most important port in East Africa. It is built on a coral island four-fifths encircled by the mainland, to which it is linked on the north side by a modern road bridge and on the south side by ferry. The bay is called *Kilindini*, which means 'place of deep water'; the name of the island, *Mombasa*, means 'island of wars'.

 ## History

From the very earliest times Mombasa – in common with the whole East African coast – has been orientated seawards, maintaining closer links with peoples across the ocean than with those of the African interior. Thanks to its particularly sheltered position, combined with easy access through a wide breach in the coral reef, vessels have been putting into the harbour since ancient times. The Greeks are believed to have berthed their ships here, followed over a period of many hundreds of years by Arabs, Indians and for a time even Chinese. Ivory and slaves were the main commodities traded on the East African coast, with the slave trade continuing to flourish well into the 19th c. The Arab coastal settlements reached their heyday in the 14th and 15th c., while the Indians came much later. The descendants of both still live here today.

The first Europeans to arrive on the East African coast were the Portuguese. In 1498 Vasco da Gama landed at Mombasa, where he was given a friendly reception before sailing on to India. Relying on a series of such bases to maintain their sea-route to India, the Portuguese established themselves in Mombasa, Malindi and elsewhere on the coast. They met with increasingly hostile resistance from the local Arab rulers, however, and in 1593 built Fort Jesus as a citadel for the defence of Mombasa and its harbour. For a

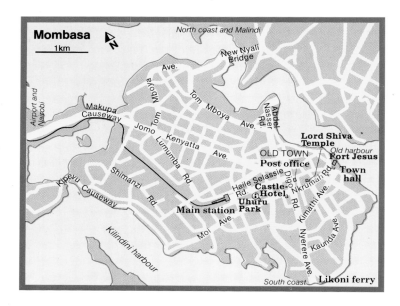

**Mombasa**
1km

North coast and Malindi

New Nyali Bridge

Ave.

Mboya

Tom Mboya Ave.

Makupa Causeway

Jomo

Tom

Kenyatta Ave.

Lumumba Rd.

Abdel Nasser Rd.

**Lord Shiva Temple**

**OLD TOWN**

Old harbour

**Fort Jesus**

**Post office**

Haile Selassie Rd.

Digo Rd.

Nkrumah Rd.

**Town hall**

Airport and Nairobi

Shimanzi Rd.

Kipevu Causeway

**Castle Hotel**

**Uhuru Park**

**Main station**

Kimathi Ave.

Moi Ave.

Nyerere Ave.

Kaunda Ave.

Kilindini harbour

South coast

**Likoni ferry**

hundred years it withstood innumerable attacks during a period of practically incessant blood-letting on both sides until, on December 13th 1698, the nine remaining members of the Portuguese garrison were finally overpowered in the fortress.

From then on Mombasa was for the most part to play an unhappy role as one of the major centres of the slave trade. In the second half of the 19th c. the British secured their sphere of influence in East Africa. Then, at the beginning of this century, Mombasa acquired renewed importance as the departure-point of the Uganda railway, vital to East African trade.

 **Sightseeing**

At the centre of the inner city is the crossroads where Nyerere Ave and Digo Rd intersect with Moi Ave and Nkrumah Rd. Most people would agree that the district bounded by Nkrumah Rd and Digo Rd is the most interesting part of Mombasa; it is certainly the oldest part.

**Old Mombasa:** Following Nkrumah Rd to its end brings you to *Fort Jesus*. At the time of its construction it was considered a perfect example of modern military architecture. Its walls in places are 2.5 m thick.

To the left of the fort is a side-street leading down to the *Old* or *Dhow Harbour*. The harbour only presents its picturesque and much-vaunted oriental spectacle in the first three months of the year. With the onset of the southern monsoon in April, the dhows set sail for their home ports on the Arabian Sea and do not reappear until the following January. The *Fish Market*, at its busiest in the early morning hours, is also at the

Old Harbour.

Now make your way through the narrow, winding alleys of the Arab quarter back to Digo Rd, at the end of which is the *Municipal Market*. Around the market the extraordinarily lively oriental-bazaar atmosphere is further heightened by the myriad aromas of Arabia. Most of the spice and perfume merchants are to be found here, as well as jewellers, money-changers and small traders dealing in a hundred different sorts of goods.

If you are interested in Hindu temples, you should make a short detour from Nkrumah Rd to the *Lord Shiva Temple* (built 1952), or else from Digo Rd to the *Jain Temple* (built 1963).

Not every temple and every mosque is worth a visit. It is the way in which Muslims, Hindus and Christians all manage to live alongside one another — taken for granted here but unusual to many visitors — that gives Mombasa its unique atmosphere. By taking your time wandering slowly through a few alleyways, you will see far more of what is special about Mombasa than by rushing along every street.

**Moi Ave and Nkrumah Rd:** The commercial life of the modern city is concentrated mainly in Nkrumah Rd and on either side of Moi Ave. Most of the shops and travel agents likely to be of interest to tourists can be found here.

Spanning Moi Ave are the massive metal elephant tusks that have become the emblem of the city. Close by are the *Information Bureau* and the *Uhuru* ('Freedom') *Gardens*, with the Uhuru Fountain in the shape of Africa, erected in 1963 when Kenya gained its independence.

The terrace of the *Castle Hotel* is a popular place for taking a breather while touring the city. From it you can watch the bustle on Moi Ave. If you have a fancy for cakes and doughnuts, you can indulge yourself at the air-conditioned *Arcade Café* in the tall building in Nkrumah Rd.

**Harbour and mainland:** There are in addition two rather special 'sights' that can be visited by taxi. The first is *Kilindini Harbour,* Mombasa's port, where, among the ocean-going ships, you can savour something of the cosmopolitan

*Mombasa*

waterside atmosphere. You apply to the security guard at the main gate for permission to enter the port area. Whether or not it is granted depends on who is on duty and what ships happen to be in port. Considerably further away, not far from the airport on the mainland, is the workshop of the *Akamba wood-carvers*. You can watch the craftsmen cutting out and carving the typical Akamba figures – and of course you can buy the figures too.

 **Mombasa at night** is also something rather special. Although the city has relatively little to offer in the way of conventional entertainment, what it does have is the harbour district with its bars and nightclubs. If you visit them you will certainly find it an experience, perhaps more of an experience than you bargained for. AIDS, incidentally, is widespread in Kenya.

*Tamarind Restaurant* (fish specialities), Cement Silos Rd in Nyali opposite the Old Harbour; *Capri Restaurant*, Ambalal House, Nkrumah Rd; *Mistral* (French), Moi Ave; *Singh Restaurant* (Indian), Mwembe Tayari Rd.

**Ex**  To Zanzibar (see page 88).

# The coast south of Mombasa

Leave Mombasa by Nyerere Ave, heading for Likoni on the far side of Kilindini Harbour. Should you be unlucky enough to find yourself stuck on the ferry in the sweltering heat, you will find ample compensation in observing the scene about you – no oriental market could be more noisily alive (passengers travel free, cars require tickets). From Likoni a good road, dead straight for most of the way, runs south to Tanzania. The distance to the border town of Lungalunga is 80 km.

In terms of popularity, the southern coast has now overtaken the holiday areas of Malindi and the coast north of Mombasa. The beaches are long, white and spacious, and the hinterland unspoiled and varied. For the last few kilometres before reaching Diani Beach, the road runs past colossal mango trees, ancient baobabs (monkey-bread trees), coconut and cashew-nut plantations and rice paddies. Delightful villages with thatched roofs cluster beneath the huge trees. People crowd around the water-sellers, and at the little markets all sorts of exotic foods can be bought (as well as potatoes and onions).

**Shelley Beach** is the first beach south of Mombasa. Turn left immediately after leaving the Likoni ferry.

**Tiwi Beach** (16 km from Mombasa) has a lovely shallow bay that is especially suitable for children.

**Diani Beach** (30 km from Mombasa) is the tourist mecca of the Kenyan coast. Along the immaculate beach the hotels lie hidden amongst palm groves and tropical gardens. The fantastic colour effects produced by the intense sunlight – and by the full moon – have given Diani Beach the reputation of being one of the most beautiful beaches in the world.

You can still watch fishermen using their ancient method of encircling fish with their nets. Nowadays, though, most of the boats are there to take tourists on trips to the reef and back.

*Ali Barbour* (full of atmosphere, in a coral grotto, with Swahili furnishings and view of the stars; from 6 pm, fish specialities); *Vulcano* (Italian).

 Casino in *Leisure Lodge*.

*Diani Beach*

 Folk evenings in the hotels and visits arranged in the neighbourhood.

  In the shopping centre on the coast road.

The *Robinson Club Baobab*, at the southern end of Diani Beach, is exceptionally well-equipped for water- and other sports.

For a long time this was the limit of tourist development, but a number of hotels have now been built further south.

**Msambweni** (45 km from Mombasa) promises much for the future. Lying off the reef is one of the best places on the whole coast for snorkelling, though it is only accessible in very calm weather. At *Seascapes* you can rent a luxury palm-thatched holiday home complete with cook. Beyond Msambweni the road runs through a sugar-cane plantation to Ramisi, where a dirt road on the left continues for the 14 km to Shimoni.

**Shimoni** ('place of the hole', 70 km from Mombasa) is a fishing village on the Pemba Channel. The potential for a deep-water harbour here seems somehow to have been overlooked. From Shimoni you can cross (20 mins) to the island of *Wasini* (pop. 500), or go on a marvellously rewarding snorkelling expedition to the *Kisite-Mpunguti Marine National Park* (1 hour).

Shimoni: *Pemba Fishing Club* (specialising in deep-sea fishing) and *Reef Fishing Lodge* (snorkelling trips and deep-sea fishing).

*Shimba Hills National Reserve*

**Vanga** (90 km from Mombasa) is the most southerly seaside destination in Kenya. This still-unspoiled fishing village – more authentically African than anywhere else on the coast – is reached by way of a poor dirt road that runs past lush banana and coconut groves. Vanga itself lies in the middle of a mangrove swamp, through which runs a narrow creek giving access to the sea.

Mangroves are very typical coastal vegetation in the tropics. The trees grow in shallow bays and estuaries, where their roots, exposed at low water, greatly impede the tidal currents and form a perfect hiding place for shellfish (large crabs, spiny lobsters, oysters). The hard trunk of the mangrove tree provides a building material used throughout East Africa and the Middle East.

## Shimba Hills National Reserve

(30 km from Mombasa; 45 minutes by car.) Ten kilometres beyond Likoni a road branches off to the right from the A 14. It makes a long arc westwards before the two roads meet again at the Tanzanian border. The main entrance to the Shimba Hills National Reserve is at Kwale, 19 km from the turn-off.

This relatively new national reserve provides a unique opportunity for watching game only half a day's excursion from Mombasa. The special attraction of the Shimba Hills is the sable antelope, which can be seen in no other conservation area in Kenya. They were introduced here some years ago and have already become well established. There are also buffalo, elephant, some lions and a number of rare species of bird.

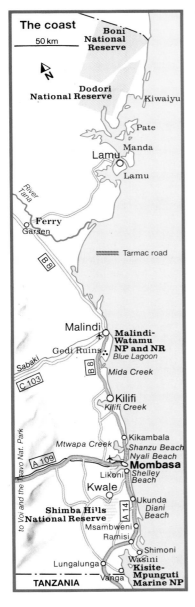

The coast

50 km

Boni National Reserve

Dodori National Reserve

Kiwaiyu

Pate

Manda

Lamu

Lamu

River Tana

Ferry
Garsen

▦ Tarmac road

B 8

Malindi

Gedi Ruins

Malindi-Watamu NP and NR
Blue Lagoon

Sabaki

C 103

B 8

Mida Creek

Kilifi
Kilifi Creek

to Voi and the Tsavo Nat. Park

A 109

Mtwapa Creek

Kikambala
Shanzu Beach
Nyali Beach

Mombasa

Likoni  Shelley Beach

Kwale

Ukunda
Diani Beach

Shimba Hills National Reserve

A 14

Msambweni

Ramisi

Shimoni

Lungalunga

Wasini

Kisite-Mpunguti Marine NP

Vanga

TANZANIA

## The coast north of Mombasa

Heading north from Mombasa, the coast road crosses the 390-m-long New Nyali Bridge.

**Nyali Beach** is the first beach north of Mombasa. Although quite close to the city, the water is clear and the beach clean. It is worth making a detour to *Mamba Village,* the largest crocodile farm in East Africa (signposted everywhere).

**Bamburi Beach** (formerly Kenyatta Beach, 13 km from Mombasa) is equally attractive, with a relatively large number of hotels. The Bamburi Cement Company works on the other side of the road cannot, fortunately, be seen from the beach. Those prone to despair about the environment will find something to hearten them right next to the cement works. Laid out across a 35-hectare tract of what was once industrial wasteland there is now a *nature trail,* a wonderful illustration of the possibilities of environmental regeneration (signposted on the B 8).

**Shanzu Beach** (20 km from Mombasa) is considered by many to be the loveliest on the north coast. Excellent hotels, including the only five-star hotel on the entire coast (*Inter-Continental*).

 Flat and spacious, with fine sand. Occasional cliffs. You can walk far out at low tide, in some places as far as the offshore coral reef.

  Deep-sea fishing, especially between August and March.

 Glass-bottomed boats.

*Le Pichet* (French restaurant; seafood specialities) on Mtwapa Bay.

 Dance evenings, folk entertainment (Giriama dancing). The hotels take turns in putting on barbecues; plus what Mombasa has to offer.

## Between Mombasa and Malindi

North of Mtwapa Creek (toll bridge), where there are one or two watersports clubs, tourist amenities thin out considerably. Near Kikambala (26 km from Mombasa) a side-road branches off to the final couple of hotels. After that the well-surfaced but little-used B 8 traverses a peaceful landscape clearly blessed with great fertility: coconut palms, pineapple and sisal plantations, and fields of maize are interspersed with giant baobab trees.

*Kilifi Creek* (58 km from Mombasa) is crossed by ferry. With time to kill before the ferry leaves, you may like to visit the *serpentarium*. But you may think it every bit as rewarding to wait aboard the ferry along with everyone else. And a tip: if you like cashew nuts, this is the place for them. You will not find fresher or cheaper cashews anywhere in Kenya.

    Deep-sea fishing; clubs for watersports on Kilifi and Mtwapa Creeks.

## Gedi National Monument

Beyond Mida Creek a small side-road branching off right towards Watamu (94 km from Mombasa) takes you to the ruins of *Gedi* or the *Gedi National Monument* as it is called.

This ruined ghost town in an ancient forest was excavated some years ago. It is still not known when the town was built, though there is a gravestone bear-ing the date 1399. It was abandoned to the jungle in the 16th c. for reasons that are also unknown. The inhabitants of the time must have engaged in thriving and far-flung trade, because finds from the excavation include everyday articles of Arabian earthenware, Indian glass and Chinese porcelain. They can be seen displayed in the little museum. Touring the ruined town reveals decayed but clearly identifiable palaces, mosques, gates and cisterns. Gedi is encircled by dense and rather eerie woodland, populated by monkeys, snakes and brightly plumaged tropical birds. Their calls seem all the louder and more exotic for being made by creatures that remain largely invisible in the trees. (Open daily 7 am–6 pm.)

## Turtle Bay, Blue Lagoon and Watamu Beach

To get to these beaches continue along the side-road off the B 8 until you come to the coast. It was here on these lovely bays with their sheltering reef that the very first beach hotels were built. It was a Garden of Eden for the Europeans in Africa long before tourism really began. Today the buildings are being modernised by the hotel companies to keep pace with the southern coast and the beaches just to the north of Mombasa.

 Flat beaches backed by cliffs, the bay being dotted with little islets.

   Deep-sea fishing.

 Glass-bottomed boats.

Return to the main B 8, from where it is 12 km to Malindi.

## Malindi Pop. 25,000

After Mombasa (120 km to the south),

*Gedi National Monument ruins*

Malindi is the second most important centre on the Kenyan coast.

 **History**

Malindi's origins still lie hidden in the darkness of the 12th and 13th c. But it is known that in the 14th and 15th c. the city state was a sultanate engaging in trade with Persia, India and even China. In 1415 Malindi presumed to honour the Emperor of China with the gift of a giraffe. The ambassador who accompanied the animal to make the presentation in Peking was personally escorted back to Malindi by a Chinese fleet under the command of an admiral! In 1498 the Portuguese seafarer Vasco da Gama, having sailed round southern Africa, came ashore here and was received with such friendliness that he was moved to name the town after his wife. The Portuguese were able to maintain their hold on Malindi with the loss of far less blood than at Mombasa. Following their final withdrawal in the 18th c. however, little was heard of Malindi – apart from its role in the slave trade –

until its rediscovery by the sun-seeking, beach-loving visitors from Europe.

 **Sightseeing**

With expectations aroused by so evocative a name, the newcomer to Malindi may at first find the reality something of a surprise, perhaps even a disappointment. Despite the shops selling souvenirs and beach gear, this small town hardly has the feel of a busy seaside resort. Malindi's nightlife, on the other hand, is certainly lively enough – though the many nightclubs and bars are centres of prostitution.

The Indian, African and Arab quarters of the town cluster tightly together, each true to differing traditions in building, customs and dress. In one you will find the low, simple, square huts of the Giriama; in another the characteristic shapes of Arab architecture; over here a mosque, there a Hindu temple, or the church of an African Christian sect; now a group of black-veiled Muslim women; next a bevy of beautiful Giriama women. This exotic and still quite unselfcon-

*Malindi Marine National Reserve*

 Diving school, snorkelling on the coral reef.

 Deep-sea fishing, especially between August and March.

 Glass-bottomed boats.

   Riding school.

 Dancing, folk entertainment (Giriama dancing), barbecues, film shows; all put on in turn by the hotels.

 *Stardust.*

## Malindi Marine National Reserve

The coral reef skirting the coast south of Malindi is a designated nature conservation area known as the Malindi Marine National Reserve. There are wonderful gardens of coral, the coral heads being gorgeously coloured and coming in all manner of shapes. The reef can be reached on foot at low water. Alternatively you can take a trip in one of the glass-bottomed boats, which also carry snorkelling gear. (The boat trips can be arranged by the hotels.)

## Lamu

With some determination you can get to Lamu by road (220 km from Mombasa, about 6 hours). The drive is interesting but tiring and can sometimes come to an abrupt halt at Garsen when the ferry over the Tana River is not operating because the river is in spate. A flight (usually from Malindi, though you can also fly direct from Mombasa or Nairobi) may not save money but it will save a lot of time. The planes are small and carry at most twelve passengers.

Lamu has acquired a growing number of almost fanatical devotees from all over the world. Even a one-day visit is

scious racial mix is what gives Malindi its special charm, a charm that is certainly not lost on the great majority of visitors.

The only monument deserving mention is the *Vasco da Gama cross*, erected by the Portuguese in 1499 on the point south of the town.

You will probably have to look twice before you notice the modern hotel zone, which also contains some luxurious private villas. It is located in the midst of lush vegetation alongside the beach to the north of the town centre. After a falling off in tourism in recent years, Malindi is now recovering again.

Almost unending, flat, with fine sand. Just north of Malindi the Sabaki River runs into the sea. After heavy rains, red laterite soil from the Tsavo National Park is carried down by the river, turning the sea a reddish-brown. When this happens it is better to swim in the hotel pool.

enough to convey some idea of the island's subtle magic, by which it contrives to cast a spell over nearly everyone who goes there. Its indefinable fascination seems to stem from the fact that, over the centuries, something novel and highly individual has grown up out of this marriage of Asia with Africa.

**Lamu** (pop. 10,000) is the chief town of the island (70 sq km) of the same name. It shares more than a thousand years of history with the islands of Manda (facing it) and Pate (to the north). From its beginnings as a base used by Arab merchants, it evolved into a trading centre maintaining lively contacts with places as far afield as China.

### The cradle of Swahili culture

It was from the mingling of Arab culture with that of the original inhabitants of the coast that Swahili culture emerged (see page 22), reaching its high point between the 12th and 15th c. Today Lamu has something of a 19th c. air about it, with no more than a hint of its earlier prosperity. The three-storeyed houses were once richly furnished with wood and fabrics. The house doors are famous for their elaborate carvings; but beds, chests and seats were also embellished in the typical Lamu style. The heights to which the art of wood carving was carried are to be seen in *Lamu Museum*, marvellously well illustrated by the two 17th c. ceremonial horns.

Twenty-four mosques from which the faithful are called to prayer five times daily are proof enough of Islam's vitality on the island. Lamu's Koranic schools have a reputation throughout the Muslim world, and every year pilgrims make their way here from all over Africa for the celebration of the Prophet's birth.

Ever since the beginning of the last century, however, the islands have been falling behind economically. The treacherous waters of the archipelago proved too hazardous for larger ships, especially for steam ships. Later, British colonial rule served only to intensify the islands' isolation. Scarcely roused even now from a lengthy slumber, they have become a promised land to the world's romantics.

Only a single car, belonging to the District Commissioner, is to be seen on Lamu's streets. Loads are transported by donkey or carried round the coast by dhow, the traditional sailing craft.

The mangoes from Lamu are known all over Kenya for their superb quality. Nowadays though it is the tourists who bring in the greatest revenue. Even so, this conservative Islamic community, standing aloof from the outside world, is strongly resistant to this growing foreign influence.

### Sightseeing

Even when flying to Lamu, you must make part of the journey by boat, since the airport is on Manda Island. The crossing by motorboat or dhow brings the added bonus of a panoramic view of Lamu.

*In Lamu*

The entire waterfront of Lamu town is one long harbour. Here porters wade waist-deep to unload cargo. Also on the waterfront is the *Lamu Museum*, definitely not to be missed. It offers a real insight into Lamu as it once was, how people dressed, what they ate and how they lived.

The town is dominated by the 20-m-tall fort, built in 1820 and until recently used as a prison. In front of the fort is the busy market place, while all around are narrow streets and the tiniest of alleys, with little shops, cafés and workshops. There is no point in having a set plan when you visit Lamu. Simply let yourself be carried along by the experience, enjoying the atmosphere.

Sad to say, the romance of Lamu is being increasingly spoiled by the carelessness with which its people dispose of their rubbish. It is piled high in the streets and along the harbour, making a playground for countless stray cats.

There is also another threat to the magic of Lamu: Kenya is proposing to build a second deep-water port on the mainland behind the island, to ease the strain on Mombasa.

A word of advice for photographers: however photogenic the women appear in their yashmaks, do not waylay them with your camera.

**Shela** (3 km south of Lamu town): This very picturesque village, complete with mosque and a number of Arab houses converted into holiday homes, can be reached on foot at low tide in about forty-five minutes, or else by dhow. The beach with its high sand-dunes seems to go on for ever, but unfortunately it offers not the least bit of shade.

 *Peponi* ('place of the wind', comfortable hotel on the ocean's edge).

 Dhow trips.

## Manda and Pate

**Takwa**, a ruined town on Manda, can be reached by dhow from Lamu. The trip involves threading a way along narrow creeks through the mangroves for about an hour – departure times are at the mercy of the tide. Takwa was abandoned by its inhabitants in the 17th c., probably because of lack of water. Today the ruins have a strangely timeless quality. On the far side of the dunes is a deserted beach with large breakers.

 *Ras Kitau*, south of Manda (organised trips for experienced divers).

**The island of Pate**, which in the 16th c. was as powerful as Mombasa and famous for its silk and its shipbuilding, lies 20 km north of Lamu. Measuring some 24 km by 7 km when the tide is out, it is reduced to only half that size at high water. A wide belt of mangroves and dangerous tidal currents make access difficult, so up to now Pate has largely been spared any tourism.

The Lamu archipelago is usually the most northerly limit for holidaymakers on the Kenyan coast. None of the safari operators will take you to the remote Dodori and Boni nature reserves on the Somali frontier, and there are still no glass-bottomed boats plying the new Kiunga Marine Reserve. There is, however, an exclusive tourist hideaway on the otherwise uninhabited island of *Kiwayu*. It can be reached only by light aircraft.

 Kiwayu Safari Village.

## Tsavo National Park

The Tsavo National Park is 2½ hours by car from Mombasa and Nairobi and is the largest reserve in Kenya. It has a 2,000-km network of tracks, more than sixty species of mammal, over five hundred different kinds of bird, and the most visitors per year of any of the Kenyan parks.

Tsavo is divided by the main Mombasa–Nairobi road into an east section and a west section. It is part of an inhospitable hinterland that was long considered uninhabitable, all the more so because the tsetse-fly prevented the Masai from grazing their cattle there.

The scenery is predominantly characterised by dry, reddish-coloured savannah on which baobab, umbrella acacia, euphorbia and stunted bush are the only plants to thrive. Also to be seen are a number of volcanic formations including extinct craters and petrified lava flows, mainly concentrated in the north-west of the park (Yatta Plateau, Chyulu Hills). The only watercourse to maintain a flow throughout the year is the Galana River, formed by the confluence of the Tsavo and Athi Rivers near Tsavo. The area to the north of the Galana River is a waterless wilderness, inaccessible and largely trackless. It can only be entered with special permission and as part of a guided group.

The park is famous for its red elephants, which enjoy dusting themselves with the red laterite soil. In the seventies they were so numerous that they had become a threat to the environment, but ·thousands then died from lack of water during two periods of drought. Highly organised game-poachers have further decimated their numbers. The scale of the poaching can be judged by the fact that from time to time the Kenyan police uncover consignments of more than 600 tusks. Rhinoceros are especially endangered. In the Far East, where ground rhino-horn is regarded as an aphrodisiac, vast sums are paid for a single horn. There are now less than 500 rhinos left in the park, despite their having been common in the early sixties.

*Cape buffalo, Tsavo National Park*

In addition to elephant, Tsavo boasts considerable numbers of buffalo, giraffe, lion, zebra and antelope, as well as monkeys. Although during the dry season it is possible to drive for long periods without seeing any animals, tracking by car along the Tsavo and Galana river-courses will usually be rewarding.

One particular area of west Tsavo has the most to offer by way of variety for a short stay, so several lodges are located there. The major attraction is *Mzima Springs*, 13 km from Kilaguni Lodge. These are fed by water from the Chyulu Hills, which then flows underground through lava tunnels before gushing out at Mzima as a crystal-clear spring with a volume of 2,250,000 litres a day. Crocodiles, hippos and several species of fish can be observed in Mzima's two pools (under the water as well, from a glass viewing-chamber).

Also easily accessible from the lodges are the *Roaring Rocks* (with an extensive view over the hills and valleys of the park), *Poacher's Look-out* near the Chyulu Gate (from which Kilimanjaro can be seen in favourable weather), and lastly *Sheitani* ('devil'), a small extinct volcano. The local people claim that strange things happen here, but the ghostly murmurings heard from time beyond recall are probably only the soughing of the wind...

 Tsavo east: *Voi Safari Lodge* (comfortable and with a swimming-pool) near Voi, quickly reached from the Mombasa road; *Tsavo Safari Camp* (good, comfortable, tented camp) by the Athi River.

 Tsavo west: *Ngulia Safari Lodge* (comfortable, on high ground with distant views, overlooking salt lick and waterholes); *Kilaguni Lodge* (water-holes). The airstrip for both lodges is at Kilaguni Lodge. Petrol and oil can be obtained here too.

*Taita Hills Lodge* with *Salt Lick Lodge* (luxurious hotel complexes situated outside the park but with their own 100-sq-km reserve teeming with game).

## From Mombasa to Nairobi

The 500 km between Mombasa and Nairobi are, of course, covered most quickly by air – between fifty and ninety minutes depending on the kind of aircraft. The two overnight trains that link the cities take either thirteen or fifteen hours. They are more than just a way of covering the distance however. One of them provides a nostalgic return to the good old days of rail travel (though the other has been somewhat modernised).

Last but not least the cross-country journey can be made by car in five to six hours. This is by no means as monotonous as might be thought and gives the traveller a real sense of distance, something that is lost to the tourist who goes by air.

Coming from Mombasa in good weather, you can see Kilimanjaro to your left for hundreds of kilometres. If you are driving, make sure you do not allow yourself to become too distracted. On the Mombasa stretch in particular keep a good look-out not only for deep pot-holes and fellow road-users with some rather original driving habits, but also for goats and cows grazing on the roadside and suddenly wandering into the carriageway. Elephant and giraffe are another hazard that may require a driver to brake sharply. Incidentally, do not pull in near the baboons squatting on the kilometre-posts in Tsavo Park. Bites and scratches are the only sort of thanks you are likely to get for feeding them.

*Nairobi from Uhuru Park*

# Nairobi Alt. 1,600–1,800 m; pop. 1.2 million

Located 120 km south of the equator, Nairobi is the capital of Kenya and the economic hub, conference centre and major crossroads of East Africa. Flights to the islands in the Indian Ocean (Madagascar, Mauritius, Réunion and the Seychelles) and to South and West Africa stop over at Nairobi. Around midnight and early in the morning, lines of jumbo jets snake across the tarmac of Kenyatta International Airport. The headquarters of the UN organisations for the environment (UNEP) and human settlement (Habitat) are in Nairobi.

 **A young capital**

Nairobi – the name means 'cool water' in the language of the Masai who once lived there – grew up at the turn of the century, starting out as a supply depot during construction of the Mombasa–Uganda railway. It was also a place where settlers could equip themselves before taking possession of land in the fertile highlands not far from the city. By the twenties Nairobi had already come to occupy a dominant position in East Africa, a position that could not be ignored by the first government of an independent Kenya. After only a little hesitation, the government declared Nairobi the capital.

 **Sightseeing**

It has to be said that there is not a great deal to see in Nairobi. It is a modern city and much like many others. Being just a hundred years old, Nairobi has no Old Town that visitors should see. Nevertheless Nairobi is an attractive and charming place because of the people who live there. They are the secret of the city's atmosphere, an atmosphere that can be felt with all five senses!

'Green city in the sun' is how Nairobi advertises itself. Some flowering shrub or other is always ablaze with colour, whether it be the red of the flame trees, the yellow of the cassias and mimosas or, most striking of all, the blue of the

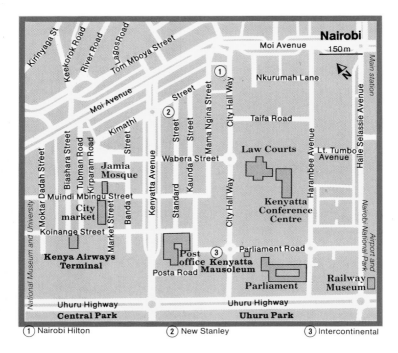

**Nairobi**

① Nairobi Hilton   ② New Stanley   ③ Intercontinental

*Jacaranda tree*

jacaranda. And always and everywhere among them bourgainvillea blooms in every conceivable shade. You will not, however, see much greenery in the city centre. Here the only things to flourish seem to be the developers.

**The commercial centre:** The business heart of the city on either side of Kenyatta Ave lies within the area bounded by Uhuru Highway and Moi Ave, City Wall Way and Moktar Dadah St. Here will be found most of the tourism-related firms: airlines and travel agents, car hire companies, jewellers, photographers and souvenir shops. Here too are many of the international hotels: the *Hilton*, the *Intercontinental* and the *New Stanley*. The *Nairobi Serena*, the historic

*Norfolk Hotel* and the exclusive *Nairobi Safari Club* in the Lilian Tower are only a few minutes' walk away. All the most expensive hotels, in other words, are found in the city centre.

It is a pity that there are so few street cafés in which to sit and enjoy Nairobi's 'champagne' climate and view the colourful bustle on the streets. The one exception is the *Thorn Tree Café* in the New Stanley. In the old days this was the place where people used to meet, and the café acted as a sort of post office. Anyone wanting to leave a message fixed it to the spiky trunk of the thorn tree. An offshoot of the tree still stands on the very same spot. Messages are no longer left on it though – after all, nowadays there is an official post office.

The *General Post Office* in fact is in Kenyatta Ave (not far from the junction with Uhuru Highway). You will find more people milling about here than almost anywhere else in Nairobi (including, alas, more pickpockets). Postal deliveries are unknown in Kenya, so a private box must be rented at the post office and checked regularly.

From the post office it is little more than a stone's throw to the *Kenyatta Mausoleum* (opposite the Intercontinental Hotel) and the *Parliament building*. Neither of these may be photographed. Parliament Rd leads to Harambee Ave, in which there are a number of government ministries and, most importantly, the *Kenyatta Conference Centre,* built by the Norwegian architect Karl Henrik Nostvik and completed in 1973. The 34-storeyed circular tower of ribbed design represents a corn cob. There is a revolving restaurant on the twenty-eighth floor. The lower building, also circular and in the style of an African hut, is the amphitheatre.

To the rear of the Conference Centre

*Moi Avenue, Nairobi*

*City Square and Kenyatta Tower*

*Jamia Mosque, Nairobi*

lies *City Square Garden*, with a monument to the first President, Jomo Kenyatta; and just north of it stand the *Law Courts*, one of the few imposing vestiges of colonial architecture.

No more than 500 m to the right from the end of Harambee Ave is Nairobi's railway station, bereft of much of its former importance. Apart from the long-distance connections to Mombasa and Kisumu (on Lake Victoria), there is now virtually no passenger traffic. Public transport has been taken over by buses and the typically Kenyan *matatus* (communal taxis). These tend to be vehicles in a dangerous state of repair, with drivers all too ready to take risks. However, they are the only form of transport to the remoter places. The stifling import restrictions on cars, with the added disincentive of customs duties and taxes totalling 260% – affecting spare parts as well – account for the fact that these heaps of scrap metal are kept running on the roads.

**Around the railway station:** Those who choose to travel from Mombasa to Nairobi by train can further indulge their nostalgia at the *Railway Museum*. It is found at the end of Station Rd, which runs in front of the railway station, and includes a collection of locomotives and carriages from the already almost legendary Uganda and Tanganyika Railway. (Open Mondays to Fridays, 8.30 am–4.30 pm.)

Also near the station – turn right down Haile Selassie Ave – is the headquarters of the *Kenya Coffee Board* (Wakulima House) where, every Tuesday, coffee is auctioned with never a single coffee bean in sight. There are coffee tastings prior to the auction but the public are excluded. Should anyone wish to watch proceedings, visits can be arranged through the Coffee Board (tel. 33 28 96).

**Old Nairobi:** Make your way along Moi Ave, past the Hilton Hotel, and back to the city centre, where the last remnants of old Nairobi can be found on the other side of Kenyatta Ave.

The large *Jamia Mosque* between Banda St and Kirparam Rd marks the transition from the anonymous façades of the modern tower blocks to the colourful streets of bazaars. The mosque, built between 1925 and 1933, can be visited by non-Muslims.

Scarcely a tourist misses the indoor *City Market* in Muindi Mbingu St, so it is perhaps no wonder that prices are high. There is a big selection of pretty baskets that are worth bargaining over.

Biashara ('Commerce') St, which crosses Muindi Mbingu St, is a lively mixture of Africa, Asia and the Far East. You can buy almost anything in the various junk shops crammed to the brim with fabrics, axes, khaki uniforms, joss sticks, digital watches and the brightly

*University, Nairobi*

coloured beads beloved of the Masai.

**The university district:** Towards the far end of Muindi Mbingu St the city bustle eases off noticeably. Across University Way, on either side of Harry Thuku Rd, is the *University*, established in the early fifties as the engineering faculty of the then combined University of East Africa. Adjoining the campus on the right-hand side of Harry Thuku St is the Norfolk Hotel. On the left is the *Kenya National Theatre*, and beyond it the exceedingly modest buildings of Kenyan radio and television, *Voice of Kenya* (VoK).

A left turn into University Way from the end of Muindi Mbingu St takes you past what today is the most exclusive place to stay in Nairobi – the *Nairobi Safari Club* in the newly built Lilian Tower. Not far away, on the corner of Monrovia St and Loita St, is the Goethe Institute, and right next to it the French Cultural Centre, which has a French restaurant. Return to Kenyatta Ave along Koinange St or Uhuru Highway.

**Uhuru Park**, on the far side of Uhuru Highway, has a small pond where boats can be hired. The park is also the venue for the Independence Day parade at which the President inspects the troops. The tall buildings on the nearby hill testify to the fact that even in developing countries governmental bureaucracy is well housed. Beware of pickpockets.

**To the north:** Since 1984 Nairobi has boasted a new 'sight', the *Jain temple* in Limuru Rd. Some 2.5 km north of the city centre (take a taxi), it is reputed to be the most beautiful such temple outside India. Built entirely in traditional style, not one piece of steel was used to tie the stonework of the walls and dome, which are richly ornamented with figures. Jainism is a form of Hinduism and shares its belief in a continuous cycle of rebirth. Visitors are allowed inside the temple.

On the way back into the city are the *National Museum* and the *Snake Park*. As well as ranging comprehensively over East African flora and fauna, the National Museum has an important prehistory section. Its exhibits relate to the very earliest history of man as revealed by finds from various archaeological

*National Museum, Nairobi*

sites in East Africa. The Snake Park contains an unusually large and therefore unusually interesting collection of African and Asian snakes; in addition there are crocodiles, lizards and tortoises. Late on Wednesday afternoons the snakes have their poison drawn off. Anyone who cares to may go along and watch. (Open daily 9.30 am–6 pm.)

The *Arboretum* (entrance in State House Ave in the north-west of the city) is an extensive wooded park where practically every kind of tree growing in East Africa can be seen and identified. (Open daily 6 am–7 pm.)

A drive through the north-eastern part of the city is only for those who feel able to confront the thought-provoking problems of the Third World while on holiday. Immediately beyond the bus station, on the far side of the Nairobi River, the city begins to fall apart. Poor residential suburbs merge imperceptibly into the Mathare Valley slums, 'home' to more than 150,000 human beings. Consideration is required here; so no photographs!

Nairobi nightlife is modest. The large hotels regularly put on both international and local entertainment.

*New Florida*, Koinange St; *Florida 2000*, Moi Ave (discos where, it is said, you will see the most beautiful girls in Africa); *Starlight Club*, Milimani Rd.

*International Casino*, Museum Hill (with floor shows and dinner).

Two drive-in cinemas (*Bellevue* and *Fox Drive-in*); also several modern cinemas.

*African Heritage*, Kenyatta Ave (art and quality handicrafts); *Gallery Watatu*, Standard St (pictures and prints); *Rowland Ward*, Standard St (ethnic handicrafts); *Cottage Craft*, Standard St (frequently has unusual handiwork by women's groups); *Undugu Shop*, Woodwale Grove in Westlands (follow Uhuru Highway in the direction of Nakuru; reasonably priced, good quality handicrafts; the proceeds go to help youths from the slums).

In addition to the larger hotels, where the week's menus often feature the cuisine of a particularly country, there are a number of foreign restaurants.

French: *Alan Bobbe's Bistro*, Koinange St; *Le Jardin de Paris*, French Cultural Centre, on the corner of Loita St and Monrovia St.

Italian: *Trattoria*, Wabera St; *Marino's Restaurant*, Mama Ngina St.

German: *Red Bull*, Mama Ngina St; *The Horseman*, out of town in Karen.

African: *African Heritage*, Kenyatta Ave (Kenyan food at midday, Ethiopian in the evening).

Chinese: *Tin-Tin*, Kenyatta Congress Centre.

Indian: *Minar*, Banda St; *Safeer*, in the Hotel Ambassadeur, Tom Mboya St.

International, but special: *Tamarind* (fish specialities), National Bank House in Harambee Ave; *Carnivore*, Langata Rd beyond Wilson Airport (a selection of meats from a large spit; you may eat as much as you like).

In Nairobi it is possible to ride as well as play golf, tennis or even polo. An introduction is needed, however, to the appropriate clubs.

*Kenya National Theatre*, Harry Thuku Rd, opposite the Norfolk Hotel; *Phoenix Players* (very small English theatre group) in Parliament Rd.

## Ex Heading south

### Nairobi National Park

Leave the city by Uhuru Highway, going past the Railway Golf Club in the direction of the airport. Immediately beyond the sports stadium, turn right into Langata Rd, which branches off to the south. On the lefthand side of the road is *Wilson Airport*, which handles safari charter flights. Just beyond its busy hangars is the little *Uhuru Garden*, conceived as a monument to Kenya's newfound statehood. There are sculptures by Kenyan artists on the themes of peace, love and unity.

Next on either side of the road come prison blocks and barracks, followed by a proliferation of new housing estates until, after about 7 km, the main entrance to Nairobi National Park is reached. (Open daily 6.30 am–7 pm; tours depart from the city centre.)

The special charm of the park is that it is almost an integral part of urban Nairobi. You can go for an afternoon walk and see game! Being only 117 sq km, it is one of the smaller national parks, but even so, except for elephant, it has pretty well everything you could wish to see: lion, rhino, buffalo, ostrich, giraffe, baboon, zebra, wildebeest, various other antelope and, in the watercourses, crocodile and hippo. If you are lucky, you could even catch sight of a cheetah.

The park is fenced on the sides skirted by roads but is open to the south, so the animals are free to come and go as they please, as befits a genuine national park. Beside the main entrance an animal orphanage has been established. Baby animals found abandoned are brought here from all over Kenya.

*Giraffe sanctuary, Nairobi*

**The Bomas of Kenya** (an open-air ethnographic museum) are situated a short distance beyond the main entrance to the national park, on the opposite side of Langata Rd. Here the life of sixteen different Kenyan peoples is reconstructed in traditional village settings. There are twice-daily performances (2.30 pm and 9 pm) which include dancing and acrobatics. Visits are arranged from Nairobi.

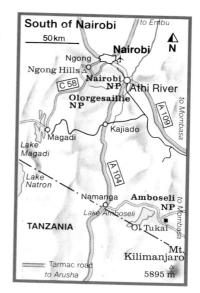

**Karen Blixen Museum:** If, having read *Out of Africa*, you have become a Karen Blixen fan, continue for another 6 km along Langata Rd to the suburb of Karen, where Karen Rd branches off left to the Karen Blixen Museum. The farmhouse that once belonged to the Danish authoress has been restored and furnished in the style of the period. From the garden there is a lovely view of the Ngong Hills and from it also, when the trees were not yet as tall, Karen Blixen could see the grave of her lover, Denys Finch-Hatton. If you want to make a pilgrimage to the grave, you should seek directions from the police in Ngong. To get to Ngong, turn left at the Karen roundabout and drive along Ngong Rd until it ends in the little town at the foot of the hills.

**The Ngong Hills** are Nairobi's emblem, and legends abound telling how they came to be formed. On the Nairobi side they rise gently; but on the far side they plunge precipitously down – sometimes 1,000 m at a time – to the *Great Rift Valley*. In Karen Blixen's time (she left Kenya in 1931) they were still densely forested. Walks on the grassy crest are definitely not to be recommended; robberies have become commonplace there.

Return to Nairobi along Ngong Rd, which goes right into the centre of the city.

### Lake Magadi
110 km; 1½ hours by car; alt. 580 m
Follow Langata Rd past the main entrance to Nairobi National Park, turning left beyond the Bomas of Kenya (see page 61) on to the tarmacked C 58 to Magadi. At first the road climbs across the slopes of the Ngong Hills before dropping some 1,300 m in stages, taking its line from the rift valley fault. With each gigantic downward step, the temperature rises noticeably and the vegetation becomes considerably poorer.

*Karen Blixen Museum*

*Ngong Hills*

The *Olorgesaillie National Park*, where many prehistoric tools have been found, is reached after 70 km. At intervals along the road, the corrugated-iron roofs of Masai villages can be seen.

Lake Magadi is visible from far off, its soda deposits glinting in the sun like fresh snow. When you reach it, the lake almost takes on the qualities of an inferno: the soda stings your nose, and with temperatures of over 40°C, the sun burns into your skin. Some Masai live in the sleepy Magadi township, but they are far outnumbered by the Soda Company's workforce.

The lake is the world's largest source of soda. Its deposits, which have been exploited since 1911, are continually replenishing themselves. The soda is transported from Magadi directly to the port of Mombasa by means of a railway line specially built for the purpose.

You can cross to the far side of the lake by the causeway, or drive down to its southern end (report to the police beforehand). At both places there are hot springs around which flamingos, pelicans and waterfowl collect. Magadi is one of the hottest places in Kenya and one of the strangest as well. There is no hotel and no filling station *en route* either, so be sure to take enough to drink with you.

## Amboseli National Park
238 km; 3½ hours by car

Drive along Uhuru Highway and past Kenyatta Airport to where the road forks not far short of the Athi River (17 km). At the fork take the road on the right, the A 104 to Namanga. It crosses a vast, often parched, grassland where, as well as Masai grazing their cattle, gazelle, zebra and giraffe can be seen. At twilight whole herds of wildebeest can suddenly stampede across the highway.

After 164 km you reach the border town of Namanga. From here the tarmac road carries on towards Tanzania's *Arusha* and the safari locations of *Ngorongoro* and *Lake Manyara* (see page 87).

**Namanga** appears to live entirely from its souvenir trade. Having survived the furious onslaught of the Masai pressing to make a sale, you must quickly regain composure because the next 75 km or so are on a really poor stretch of road: treacherous loose sand, a surface rippled like a washboard, and plenty of dust to choke on. In the rainy season *Lake Amboseli* will be seen stretching away into the distance from immediately beyond the park entrance (the only building for miles around). The water can cover as much as 114 sq km

*Amboseli National Park*

— only for it to disappear again in the dry season. If you then drive across the dried-out lake bed, you will see mirages on every side.

**Amboseli** was once the jewel among Kenya's national parks. Now however it appears to be heading inescapably towards ecological disaster. Since 1985 whole forests have disappeared, leaving only a few huge old acacias surviving. The entire park is rapidly becoming little more than a wilderness, and at a frightening pace.

One reason is a rise in the water-table, which has caused large tracts of ground to become saline. In these places not even grass will grow any more. Also to blame are elephant herds that have grown, through over-zealous protection, far beyond a size sustain-able by the small park. They trample down every bush and flatten every tree.

And lastly there are simply too many tourists. Amboseli, within easy reach of Mombasa and Nairobi, attracts 100,000 visitors a year. In their eagerness to display its wealth of animals, the safari buses plough up the park's terrain (even though, minor detours apart, they are restricted to the designated trails).

These environmental changes have already had their effect on the wildlife. The handsome, dark Amboseli lions have grown indifferent to the noise of the buses besieging them. A lot of giraffe and gazelle have retreated into the surrounding scrubland, though in the dry season they return in search of water in Amboseli's swamps. At that time of year the reserve can still claim the densest concentration of animals in

Africa. Photographers can be sure of getting at least four of the 'big five' (i.e. rhino, buffalo, lion and elephant) within range of their viewfinders.

The most frequently photographed subject of all, however, is the snow-capped Kilimanjaro, almost 6,000 m high – if, that is, Africa's highest mountain makes itself visible at all. The best times are in the early morning and evening.

**Ol Tukai,** inside the park, is a visitors' centre with filling station, simple self-catering huts (no shopping facilities) and two lodges (hotels). Park rangers are also based there.

The Masai are seldom seen in Amboseli. They are not allowed to bring their herds into the park, although it is hard for them to understand why the precious water should be reserved for the wildlife, especially in times of drought. In compensation they profit directly from the park fees, which flow into their district coffers.

 *Amboseli Serena* (a hotel complex of interesting design, which combines elements of the Masai *manyatta* with European comfort; floodlit water-hole to which the animals are lured); *Amboseli Lodge*, the heart of Ol Tukai (detached wooden huts); *Kilimanjaro Safari Lodge* (next to Amboseli Lodge; circular layout, comfortable wooden huts, fantastic view of the mountain); *Kilimanjaro Buffalo Lodge* (outside the park on the way to Loitokitok); *Kimana Lodge* (in a well-wooded area outside the park, lots of Masai *manyattas* all around).

 In all the lodges.

 Ol Tukai has an airstrip for light aircraft. Petrol and oil available.

## **Ex** Heading west

### Mayer's Farm and Masai Mara Game Reserve

Leave the city centre by Uhuru Highway, driving in the direction of Nakuru. The A 104 to Nakuru is Kenya's main traffic artery and is extremely busy. Slow tanker lorries *en route* to Uganda, Ruanda and Burundi hold up the traffic as well as thoroughly polluting the atmosphere.

The countryside here is thickly populated and every square metre of ground is intensively cultivated right up to the roadside. To tourists the Kikuyu's fields tend to look disorganised. Maize, beans, potatoes and bananas grow in apparent confusion, and the soil is only crudely broken up. But now development aid workers have also come to recognise the advantages of this method of cultivation. For one thing the ground is protected from excessive water loss; for another the mixed cropping increases the chances of at least one type of plant yielding well.

Altogether it is 40 km to the escarpment where the highlands drop down 600 m into the Great Rift Valley.

**Mayer's Farm** (60 km): Before the A 104 reaches the bottom of the valley, a bush road turns sharply off to the left to Mayer's Farm (5 km from the turn-off). The 2,230-ha cattle ranch extends from the slopes of the escarpment far into the Rift Valley below. It was opened to the public by the owners some years ago. There is no longer general access, however, to the particularly lovely gardens, which are watered by warm springs.

**Masai Mara Game Reserve** (266 km, 5 hours by car from Nairobi): Where

*Masai Mara giraffe*

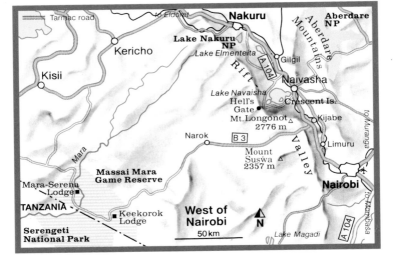

the A 104 meets the valley floor, a small chapel can be seen on the right. It was erected by Italian prisoners engaged in road construction here during the Second World War.

At Kijabe turn left on to the tarmacked B 3. A few kilometres along it on the left-hand side stands the Longonot satellite station, which handles radio and telephone transmissions to and from Europe. Also on the left is *Mount Suswa*, a 2,357-m-high volcano. Many Masai are encountered with their herds before you reach Narok (146 km from Nairobi), a thriving Masai settlement. From there the route continues on tracks that can become impassable during the rainy season, surely one of the reasons for the increasing popularity of air safaris. Of all Kenya's reserves, the Mara possesses the greatest abundance of game. It forms a single ecological unit with Tanzania's Serengeti, the animals moving freely back and forth between the two countries. The peak of the migrations occurs at the beginning of August, with the northwards journey of more than a million wildebeest and zebra, travelling in seemingly endless ranks. The Mara River flows red with the blood of animals ambushed by the crocodiles that lie in wait for them at the crossings. A great many animals also drown while fording the river. The wildebeest and zebra are driven north into Kenya by drought; there they give birth to their young, returning to Tanzania with them in October and November.

Even outside the migration period, however, the Mara is unique: gentle hills where the grass billows like cornfields, scattered areas of tropical river forest, and a superabundance of wildlife. Luck must really be against anyone who leaves without sighting a lion or leopard here – the Masai Mara Game Reserve can claim the largest lion population in Kenya. Depending on the season, elephant too are encountered everywhere, while the buffalo herds run to 200 or more animals. Only the rhino are scarce, having been hunted almost to extinction by poachers. The surviving animals are now kept under constant surveillance.

Driving cross-country is still allowed in the Mara (though it is essential to take a guide). There are other options available, however, for example a trek on horseback lasting several days (only for really good riders), and two- to four-day safaris on foot, sleeping out almost anywhere under nothing more than a mosquito net. Some of the camps also arrange short game-walks and night-drives, with searchlights to spot animals that are otherwise almost never seen (porcupine, jumping hare, bat-eared fox). The Mara's speciality, though, is its balloon safaris. Enormous hot-air balloons, carrying a maximum of twelve passengers in their baskets, take off from near the lodges at sunrise to drift silently over the landscape and the animals, silently that is except for the sporadic hissing of the gas burners. The direction of flight is determined by the wind, and on landing – after about an hour in the air – a champagne breakfast is waiting, set up by a ground crew who have followed in jeeps. Of course, this unusual way of seeing game has a price.

There are only three lodges in the reserve itself: *Keekorok*, with cottages and luxury tents, where Kenya's state visitors also stay (normal mortals then have to vacate the area); the *Mara Serena Lodge*, situated high above the Mara River, a complex with Masai style accommodation; and the *Mara Sopa Lodge*.

There are a number of camps located along the boundary of the reserve, some of which, *Intrepids Club*,

*Governor's Camp* and *Kichwa Tembo Camp* in particular, are very luxurious. Others include *Sarova Camp, Cottar's Camp, Mara Buffalo, Fig Tree* and *Mara River Camp.*

✈ There are airstrips at Keekorok, Governor's Camp, Mara Serena and Intrepids (45 min from Nairobi, about 90 min from Mombasa).

## Lake Naivasha
90 km; 1½ hours; alt. 1,700 m

To make this very worthwhile one-day excursion, leave Nairobi on the A 104 as if heading for the Masai Mara. Instead of turning off for Narok, however, carry straight on in the direction of Limuru. The road then follows the line of the escarpment, with one marvellous view after another across the Rift Valley. Still at over 2,000 m of altitude, it passes through dense coniferous forests and moorland. Away to the right rise the

*Aberdares*, and beyond them, in clear weather, *Mount Kenya's* glaciers shine. There is a viewpoint (signposted) from which you can look over to *Longonot crater* (2,776 m) and *Lake Naivasha* itself.

After this the road drops steeply down to the valley floor. Sometimes you will meet with herds of giraffe crossing the highway, and always there are farmers at the roadside selling potatoes, cabbages, carrots, rhubarb, pears, plums and sheepskins.

Lake Naivasha is a genuine freshwater lake in the Rift Valley. It is alive with fish and freshwater crabs, and there is an abundance of birdlife to delight the keenest ornithologist. The hotels hire out boats, so you can search out waterfowl in the reeds or cormorant colonies in dead trees in the lake. Alternatively, a ferry will take you over to *Crescent Island*, a private bird sanctuary

*Lake Naivasha*

*The Rift Valley*

where waterbuck, Thomson's gazelle and zebra also frisk about (but there are snakes too).

Since it can be irrigated throughout the year, the land immediately around the lake is used for intensive market gardening. The matchstick-thin Kenya beans come from here, as do artichokes, peppers, strawberries and melons. Also here is the world's biggest carnation nursery, where every day a million blooms are cut for immediate export to Europe.

 *Lake Naivasha Hotel* (in the park right next to the lake, beautifully kept, with swimming-pool); *Safariland Lodge* (club complex with riding and swimming-pool, fairly simple rooms).

**Ex** **Hell's Gate** makes an interesting outing. From the south shore of the lake you drive along a narrow track past steep cliffs – haunt of the rare lammergeyer, a bearded vulture – to the *Njorowa Gorge* (c. 8 km). Nearby are hot springs, some as hot as 300° C, the steam hissing from the ground. Some of this geothermal heat is already being harnessed to produce energy.

**Mount Longonot** looks just like a model of a volcano when seen from the road above the escarpment. From Naivasha it is reached by the road along the valley floor. The car can be taken right to the foot of the mountain (where somebody should be left behind to keep watch on it). About an hour's steep climb brings you to the crater rim, to be rewarded with a long view down into the valley and another into the depths of the vertically-sided crater. Allow about three hours for walking round the crater (and remember to take something with you to slake your thirst in hot weather).

*Flamingos, Lake Nakuru*

## Lake Nakuru National Park

**157 km from Nairobi; alt. 1,860 m**
Since the road to Nakuru was completed as part of the Trans-African Highway, the world-famous Lake Nakuru bird sanctuary can easily be visited on a day-trip from Nairobi.

Beyond Naivasha the road runs through a forest of umbrella acacias before the terrain changes to become bare and monotonous. On the left, a little beyond the small garrison town of Gilgil (2,030 m), is the smallest soda lake in the Rift Valley, *Lake Elmenteita*, the shores of which are often aglow with the pink of flamingos. The 25-sq-m lake is privately owned by the heirs of Lord Delamere, the best-known pioneer of British settlement in Kenya. Further on, with the town of Nakuru in sight, turn off left to the Lake Nakuru National Park.

The park takes in the lake and the adjoining lakeside area. At only 202 sq km it is one of the smallest of Kenya's national parks, yet it is also one of the most interesting.

In the early eighties Lake Nakuru was the setting for several films about Africa. The flamingo colonies alone, strung like pink beads along the edge of the lake, are enough to send viewers into raptures. In fact this 'unspoiled world' had to be regenerated by cleaning the lake of effluent.

Holding their own with the army of flamingos — sometimes counted in their millions — are the cohorts of pelicans, bulky birds by comparison. None of the other 400 species represented in the park are found in such numbers. Even so, cormorants, storks, herons, ibises, ospreys, buzzards and falcons are plentiful. In addition many migratory birds from Europe spend the winter here.

In recent years Lake Nakuru, like all the lakes in the Kenyan Rift Valley, has shrunk considerably. An area many hundreds of metres from the present shoreline now lies waste; nothing will grow as yet on the saline ground.

Nakuru nevertheless is rapidly becoming a reserve for the rest of Kenya's game as well. There are already far too many waterbuck; impala, Thomson's gazelle and warthog are also very numerous. In the scrub and woodland at the south end of the park there are giraffe, zebra and cheetah. Now that the park has been completely enclosed, rhino are being introduced.

 *Lake Nakuru Lodge*; *Lion Hill Camp* (comfortable bungalows).

**The town of Nakuru** (pop. 105,000) grew up, as did Nairobi, when the railway was being built. From the Uganda (Kampala) main line, a branch diverts here to Kisumu on Lake Victoria. During the colonial period, Nakuru was the agricultural capital of Kenya, and even today the silhouettes of the grain silos dominate the skyline of the country's fourth largest town. *State House*, on the right-hand side as you enter Nakuru, is one of the President of the Republic's official residences.

*Looking towards Mount Kenya from 'Treetops'*

# Between the Great Rift Valley and Mount Kenya

There can be few landscapes more exciting than that of the territory between the Rift Valley lakes on the one hand and the Mount Kenya massif and Aberdare Mountains on the other. A safari here in the north-west focuses on a land of contrasts: of alpine flora and sparse scrub, of glaciers and hot sulphur springs, of fertile farmland and lava rubble. Here you can meet farmers who cultivate their land with European machinery, and nomads who drive their camels to ancient rhythms across the heat-shimmering plain.

## Mount Kenya and the Aberdares

The area around Mount Kenya and the Aberdares is the true heart of Kenya, and many Kenyans have a strong emotional attachment to this particular bit of their country. It is here, so the Kikuyu believe, that God resides when he is on earth; it is here that many of the myths that are so much a part of the history of Kenya's tribes are set; and it was here that the struggle for freedom against the colonial power was centred, memories of which linger on in the minds of the rural population especially. Here most of the rain so vital to life in Kenya falls, and here too are found the sources of those few rivers on which the desert nomads of Kenya's west and north rely.

Leaving Nairobi, the route follows the Thika road, passing the golf club, Utalii College (Kenya's hotel-catering college), the athletics stadium (built with Chinese help) and Kenyatta University College.

**Thika** Alt. 1,490 m; pop. 45,000

Thika (40 km from Nairobi) is fast developing into an industrial centre (textiles, paper, lorry assembly and canned foods). Its immediate surroundings, on the other hand, take their character from a vast pineapple plantation. The town was made famous by Elspeth Huxley's book *The Flame Trees of Thika*, in which she wrote about the early days of white settlement. Also dating from this time is the Blue Post Hotel, on the right-hand side of the A 2. From the garden there is a lovely view of the *Chania Falls*.

**Fourteen Falls**, a classic African backdrop reminiscent of a Tarzan film, warrants a short detour. Leave Thika in the direction of Garissa, turning off after 13 km on to a dirt road which, after about another 9 km, brings you to a bridge over the Athi River. The falls themselves are a few hundred metres

downstream. Rising high on the other side of the river is *Kilimambogo* (Buffalo Mountain, 2,146 m), which has been designated a national park. As its name suggests, buffalo roam in its forest.

North of Thika the A 2 runs through the former 'White Highlands', past coffee, tea and sisal plantations, and across the Tana River, which flows on eastwards to become Kenya's largest river. In fine weather the peak of Mount Kenya can be seen glistening ahead, now to one side of the road, now to the other. At Sagana the road to Embu branches off to the right. If you are making the drive all the way round the mountain, this is the route by which you will return.

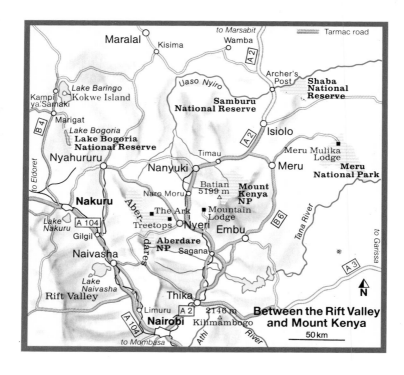

**Nyeri** Alt. 1,800 m; pop. 40,000
Nyeri, 153 km from Nairobi, is the administrative capital of Central Province. In its vicinity are various lodges from which you can explore the *Aberdare National Park* and the *Mount Kenya Park*. Additionally, in Nyeri itself there is the *Outspan Hotel*, in the grounds of which stands the cottage formerly belonging to the founder of the Scout movement, Lord Baden-Powell, who died there in 1941.

**Treetops:** It is from the Outspan that visitors make the trip to the legendary Treetops Hotel. Here, in 1952, the then Princess Elizabeth was informed of her father's death and her accession to the throne. This piece of history has proved a gold-mine for the owners. After the original lodge – built to accommodate big-game hunters – was destroyed by the Mau Mau, a wooden hotel for 73 guests was erected on the same spot. Elephant, buffalo, rhino and waterbuck can be viewed by floodlight, though what you actually see is rather a matter of luck.

Visits to Treetops begin with lunch at the Outspan, followed by Kikuyu dancing and the chance to have your fortune read from a calabash by a medicine man. Next comes the transfer to Treetops by bus, with the last part of the journey (20 mins) having to be made on foot. If you do not want to stay up the whole night, you can arrange to be woken if and when a 'big' animal appears. Breakfast is back at the Outspan.

**The Ark:** The Treetops recipe for success has since been copied. In The Ark's case a further important ingredient has

*Treetops Hotel*

been added: a certain exclusiveness. It is run in conjunction with the *Aberdare Country Club*, a former country house occupying a beautiful situation 15 km north of Nyeri. Something else rather special here are the bongo, excessively shy, reddish-coloured antelope which, given luck, can sometimes be glimpsed. The Ark has, of course, a water-hole to which game is lured. In addition to all this, the Country Club is a base for guided hill-walking in the Aberdares.

**Mountain Lodge,** on the slopes of Mount Kenya opposite, is the area's third treetop hotel. This too has a water-hole and is sited in dense forest at a height of 2,100 m, on a long-established elephant path. It can be reached directly by car.

As a rule none of the treetop hotels admits small children. Take warm clothes. They are essential, especially in the cold months of June to August – not for nothing do you find a hotwater-bottle waiting in your room.

### Aberdare National Park
175 km; alt. 3,000–4,000 m
The park in some ways seems most

un-African; its high-lying moorland and waterfalls, its lichens and heathers, and its often misty skies are somehow more in keeping with northern Europe. But elephant, leopard, buffalo, rhino and great forest hogs soon reveal its true provenance. The inaccessible forests covering the flanks of the mountains provided safe refuge for the Mau Mau during the rebellion. Even today caches of weapons are believed to be hidden there. Only one road cuts right through the park, connecting Nyeri and Naivasha (115 km). When it rains, it becomes impassable even with four-wheel drive; for an ordinary saloon car, a light shower can threaten disaster.

## Naro Moru 190 km

Most parties setting off to climb Mount Kenya start out from this small settlement on the Nanyuki road. You can hire porters and guides here, or have the whole climb organised for you.

 *Naro Moru River Lodge* (cottage-style hotel with a base camp for climbers).

 All the necessary equipment for climbing, including tents and cooking pots, can be hired.

 Trout in the Naro Moru River.

## Mount Kenya National Park

The park boundary is some 20 km from Naro Moru (dirt road). At the gate you can reserve a bed in the *Meteorological Station* (at 3,000 m) or the *Mackinder's Camp* bunkhouse. A night at the Met Station is advisable if you are not yet acclimatised. It is situated in dense rain forest where buffalo, elephant, mountain leopard and monkeys mean that caution is required. Next morning a four- to five-hour climb brings you to Mackinder's Camp (4,200 m). Anyone with energy left can go walkabout in the botanically fascinating high-level valley. Rock hyrax, marmot-like creatures very closely related zoologically to the elephant, scamper about under giant lobelia and giant groundsel.

The ascent of *Point Lenana* (4,985 m) begins at about three in the morning, when the steep scree slopes below the glacier are still frozen solid. The summit of the massif's third highest peak should be reached by sunrise. The descent to the Meteorological Station and return to Naro Moru can then be completed the same day.

The two highest peaks, *Batian* (5,199 m) and *Nelion* (5,188 m) — both, like Lenana, named after Masai leaders — can only be tackled by experienced mountaineers. Another option is to go round Mount Kenya on foot, which takes three to six days.

Although climbing Point Lenana requires no mountaineering skills, the lack of oxygen at such a height is very punishing, especially if you engage in anything particularly strenuous. Medical advice should definitely be taken in advance. At the first signs of altitude sickness (dizziness, headache, nausea) you should descend at once.

It has to be emphasised as well that the mountain-rescue arrangements do not bear comparison with those in other parts of the world. At 4,000 m very low temperatures prevail even on the equator, and to venture up ill-prepared is simply to invite disaster.

If you are not passionately enthusiastic about climbing, there are other rather more comfortable ways in which you can still gain enjoyment from Kenya's highest mountain. You should keep going northwards on the A 2.

# Nanyuki

215 km; alt. 1,950 m; pop. 20,000

Nanyuki at one time was a centre for European settlers. Immediately before entering the town you find yourself crossing the equator – marked by a sign at the roadside and some souvenir stalls. The town itself has little to offer in the way of tourist attractions, but directly on entering it, you will find a road branching off to the right to the *Mount Kenya Safari Club* (10 km).

The Club (2,300 m) is still one of the most select places to stay in Kenya, even if it is not quite as exclusive as it used to be. A film studio in the spacious grounds is a reminder that William Holden was among those who founded the Club in 1959. Anyone choosing to spend a few days relaxing here will find facilities for several different kinds of sport.

The Club has strict rules. Children under twelve are not permitted to dine with their parents in the evening, and jacket and tie are obligatory even for boys over twelve.

At Nanyuki the road branches: the right fork continues round Mount Kenya; the left one leads to Nyahururu and on round the Aberdares.

# Nyahururu

Alt. 2,360 m; pop. 13,000

Formerly known as Thomson's Falls, Nyahururu is 94 km from Nanyuki. It is the hub of a large farming area interrupted by extensive forests and high-lying moorland. The 73-m-high falls, which once gave the town its name, were discovered in 1883 by the Scottish geologist Joseph Thomson. He was the first European to journey by direct route from Mombasa to the northern side of Lake Victoria, cutting right across the feared Masai country. The Thomson's gazelle is also named after him.

From Nyahururu the road descends to Gilgit and from there via Naivasha back to Nairobi.

If you decide instead to drive round Mount Kenya, follow the A 2 east from Nanyuki. The road, climbing continuously, crosses a fertile landscape with large ranches, where the finest cattle in Kenya are reared and wheat fields stretch as far as the eye can see.

 *Kentrout*, just outside the little town of Timau (a small garden-restaurant serving fresh trout from the grill; trout ponds).

# Meru Alt. 1,580 m; pop. 77,000

The town of Meru, situated some 269 km from Nairobi in an area of rich farmland, serves as a sort of capital to the Meru people. From here it is another 76 km to the national park.

# Meru National Park

This was the home of Elsa, the famous lioness whose story became known the world over through Joy Adamson's books and films. The Meru's real attraction, however, is its rare white rhino. Compared to their dangerous cousins the black rhino, white rhino are altogether better natured. Also special are the reticulated giraffe and Grevy's zebra, both rare. They share the park with the usual elephant, buffalo, antelope, gazelle, waterbuck and warthog. The Meru is equally well known for its variety of birdlife.

North of the Rojeweru River – passable only with difficulty during the rainy

*Zebra, Meru National Park*

season – the terrain is open savannah. The southern part of the park on the other hand is covered with thick thorn-bushes, while the lush banks of the Tana River are a rich source of succulent fodder for hungry animals.

🛏 *Meru Mulika Lodge*, a delightful place, with swimming-pool and an airstrip for light aircraft.

## Lake Baringo and Samburu

At least four days should be set aside for a safari to the fascinating Rift Valley lakes and Samburu Game Reserve. The trip may seem something of a diversion from the business of touring the 'big' parks, but you will certainly find plenty of photographic opportunities. The Samburu has all the 'usual' game animals and some unusual ones as well: gere-nuk, reticulated giraffe and Grevy's zebra. And you will glimpse a part of Africa still largely untouched by Euro-pean influence.

Setting out from Nairobi, take the A 104 via Limuru and Naivasha to Nakuru. At Nakuru a good road, the B 4, branches off north to Marigat. The distance (from Nairobi) to Lake Baringo on the floor of the Great Rift Valley is 274 km.

## Lake Baringo

The lake, at an altitude of 975 m, covers some 130 sq km and is nowhere deeper than 30 m. It has no known outlet, and the earth washed into it by the rains gives it its brownish colour. Although hippo and crocodile wallow in its slightly brackish water, many tourists still ven-ture in to bathe and waterski.

The locals use dugouts or tiny papy-rus craft, but tourists will find motor-boats available to explore the banks of reeds rich in birdlife. There are also guided walks through the bush with an ornithologist, an opportunity to observe the birds in the company of an expert.

About 2 km from the tiny township of Kampi ya 'Samaki is the snake farm belonging to Jonathan Leakey, son of the famous archaeologist husband-and-wife team, who supplies snakes and other reptiles to zoos throughout the world. You can watch the snakes being milked of their poison to provide serum.

A visit to a *Njemps manyatta* is also worth while if you want to take photos. The Njemps are a people related to the Masai.

For the moment Lake Baringo leads the field in the contest for the title of 'the cradle of mankind'. A jaw-bone found there in 1984 is believed to be almost five million years old, which would make it the oldest of all human remains yet discovered and a renewed indication that mankind originated in Africa.

 *Lake Baringo Club*, right next to the lake; *Island Camp* (comfortable tented camp) on Ol Kokwa island in the middle of the lake.

## Ex Lake Bogoria National Reserve

Lake Bogoria (formerly Lake Hannington) is a soda lake set in a supremely beautiful location 30 km (dirt road) from Lake Baringo. Only 10 km long and 5 km wide, it is one of the smallest national parks but also one of the most unusual. Its shores are crowded with thousands of flamingos, which feed on algae in the shallow water. This is the only place in Kenya where flamingos breed, their main breeding ground being Lake Natron in Tanzania.

Even more special to Lake Bogoria, however, are its geysers and hot springs. Jets of boiling water spout from the earth right beside the lake shore. The water is hotter than it looks, so you would be wise not to venture too close – the ground around can be treacherous too.

The tarmac road ends just beyond Lake Baringo. The route then continues to Maralal on a very dusty track.

## Maralal Alt. 1,985 m; pop. 10,000

This colourful little town is situated in the midst of a game sanctuary. As a result it is quite usual for zebra and buffalo to be seen grazing in its gardens. Maralal's 'main street', with its ramshackle shops selling just about everything, is undoubtedly one of the most photogenic spots anywhere in Kenya. But it mostly owes its atmosphere to the brightly decked Samburu warriors who are not at all happy to be photographed. Simply looking about you for a while and enjoying your surroundings will make for a more agreeable experience here than trying to outwit the Samburu. The Samburu people are closely related to the Masai, being confusingly like them in appearance and sharing many of the same traditions.

 Maralal Safari Lodge (leopards!).

## Samburu and Shaba National Reserves

From Maralal return along the track to Kisima, heading first for Wamba and then on to *Isiolo*. At *Archer's Post*, before you reach Isiolo, there is a choice of two game reserves, the Samburu Reserve on the right and the Shaba Reserve on the left. In both, life is entirely dependent on the Uaso Nyiro River, one of the few watercourses in the north of Kenya that is not seasonal. Apart from the luxuriant vegetation near the river, thornbush savannah predominates. There are elephant, reticulated giraffe, gerenuk, Grevy's zebra, lion and leopard. Of the two reserves, only Samburu is at all well geared to tourists.

*Grevy's zebra, leopard, crocodile and reticulated giraffe in Samburu Reserve*

🛏️ Samburu: *Samburu Game Lodge* and *Samburu Serena Lodge* (both put down bait to lure crocodile and leopard); *Buffalo Springs Tented Lodge*; *Larson's Camp*.

🛏️ Shaba: *Sarova Shaba* (luxury lodge).

**Isiolo** Alt. 1,200 m; pop. 12,000

Isiolo, delightfully outlandish, is the last outpost of civilisation before the remote deserts of the north. It is also the furthest south the desert nomads venture with their camel herds.

Isiolo's more distant environs can be explored by camel on a surprisingly comfortably safari, the brainchild of a former big-game hunter. A week is spent riding or walking through the virgin scrub, sleeping under the stars covered only by a mosquito net. (Book through Nairobi travel agencies.)

From Isiolo continue on the now excellent A 2, which climbs steadily towards Mount Kenya. The great contrast between the cool green heights of the Mount Kenya massif and the boundless heat-shimmering plain is quite unforgettable.

There are now two possibilities. One is to return to Nairobi direct via Nanyuki and Nyeri. Still open to you, however, is the opportunity to drive round Mount Kenya from the north (the turn-off is 22 km beyond Isiolo), visiting the Meru National Park on the way (see page 75).

The B 6, which skirts the eastern side of the mountain *en route* via Embu to Sagana, is also a first-class road.

# The north

Further to the north of Mount Kenya there is really nothing. Desert and semi-desert stretch the whole way to Ethiopia and the Sudan, dotted only with a handful of tiny oases. It is hard to believe that anyone can exist here. Yet hundreds of thousands manage to do so, moving freely across national boundaries with their herds of camels and goats.

For many devotees of Kenya, the barren north is the real Kenya. Up to 1963 the British colonial administration closed off this whole area. The tribes who lived here were considered primitive and beyond improvement. It was only after Kenya became independent that the first missionaries were allowed among the people and the affairs of the region were subject to regulation for the first time by officials of the fledgeling state. So it is not surprising that the need for schools, hospitals and roads is greater here than anywhere else in Kenya. Nor is it any wonder that educated Kenyans still strive to avoid being posted to this far-flung part of their country.

Today a drive up to the north remains an adventure. There are indeed now some lodges, and some stretches on the way are recognisable as roads. But there are still 1,500 km of track to be covered, not exactly a picnic. Four-wheel drive, ample supplies of drinking water and petrol and, above all, plenty of time are all essential. Not even a Land Rover will average any great speed on lava terrain and breakdowns must be allowed for – as must the rains, which, though rare, are so violent that dry river beds can become raging torrents in a matter of minutes.

*Turkana fishermen in Lake Turkana*

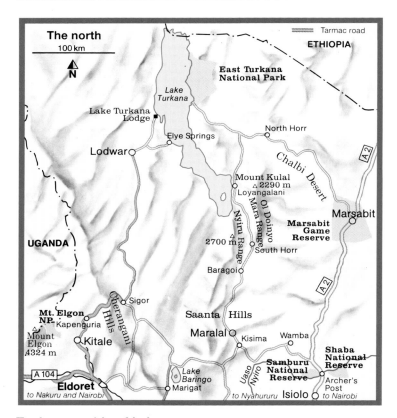

## The north

100 km

N

Tarmac road

**ETHIOPIA**

*Lake Turkana*

**East Turkana National Park**

Lake Turkana Lodge

Elye Springs

**Lodwar**

North Horr

*Chalbi Desert*

A 2

Mount Kulal
△ 2290 m
Loyangalani

*Nyiru Range*

*Ol Doinyo Mara Range*

2700 m

**Marsabit Game Reserve**

**Marsabit**

South Horr

Baragoi

A 2

**UGANDA**

*Cherangani Hills*

Sigor

Mt. Elgon NP.
△ Kapenguria
Mount Elgon 4324 m

○ Kitale

*Saanta Hills*

**Maralal** ○ Kisima

Wamba

**Shaba National Reserve**

A 104

*Lake Baringo*
○ Marigat

**Eldoret** ○
*to Nakuru and Nairobi*

*Uaso Nyiro*

**Samburu National Reserve**

Archer's Post

*to Nyahururu* Isiolo ○ *to Nairobi*

## To the east side of Lake Turkana

Nairobi is once again the departure-point for this safari. Take the A 104 via Naivasha to Nakuru, then the B 4 to Lake Baringo and on to Maralal (see page 76). Beyond Maralal the track at first crosses the cool green uplands of the *Saanta Hills,* before dropping down gradually to the hot dry plain. After 97 km you reach *Baragoi,* an attractive small settlement. Petrified wood is found nearby and offered for sale to tourists.

**South Horr,** the loveliest oasis in Kenya, is some 40 km further on. Wedged between the Nyiru (2,700 m) and Ol Doinyo Mara ranges is an ever-green forest extending over several kilometres and teeming with game. The settlement itself consists of little more than a Catholic mission, a school and a hospital.

 *Kurungu Camp*, about 10 km beyond South Horr; not always open.

Seventy kilometres of track follow, most of them across black lava. The roughest spots have been paved with cement, but this is still a stretch to shred tyres. From time to time you come across nomads with sizeable herds of camels. Then, all of a sudden, Lake Turkana stretches out at your feet.

**Lake Turkana:** From the moment you set eyes on it you need no telling why the 230-km-long lake is also called the Jade Sea. The first European to catch sight of it shimmering from afar was an Austrian, Count Teleki, in 1887. He named it Lake Rudolph after his country's Crown Prince.

With its play of hues — jade water, blue sky, black lava, and white, yellow and green volcanic rock — the lake has ever since held an extraordinary fascination for Europeans.

To add to the searing sun (take protective creams and clothing!) a strong wind blows almost continuously over Lake Turkana. The water is very alkaline, so it feels soapy. While there is no risk of bilharzia, there are plenty of crocodiles. These are said to feed so well on fish that they have no interest in humans, but it is obviously wise to take the greatest possible care.

The Turkana people after whom the lake is now named are the most warlike in Kenya. Estimated to number some 260,000, they have indescribably hard lives. They are semi-nomads, living mainly from their sheep, goats and especially their camels. During the rainy season, however, the women plant small fields of millet and pumpkins along river beds and in hollows. Walking 60 km a day (barefoot over jagged lava and prickly thorns) presents no problem to a Turkana. Raids on cattle belonging to neighbouring tribes are still the order of the day, and not infrequently a herds-

*Lake Turkana*

man's life is taken in the process. The cattle thieves are able to cover their tracks easily enough in the desert. The circular wrist-knives worn by the Turkana are very much feared.

**Loyangalani** ('the place of many trees') is the only oasis on the eastern side of the lake and offers the only possibility for an overnight stay. It is about 2 km inland, at a spot where an abundance of warm, fresh water comes bubbling out of the ground. Around the Italian Catholic mission the Turkana have built their circular palm-leaf huts. There is an airstrip for the charter planes from Nairobi (the flight takes 1½ hours) bringing short-of-time anglers to fish the lake for the magnificent Nile perch, which can weigh anything up to 100 kg. Most of the area around the hot springs has been taken over by the Oasis Club, where the hard leaves of the enormous borassus palms creak deafeningly in Turkana's notorious night-time wind storms.

 *Oasis Club* (a full day's subscription must be paid even if you only want a beer; two swimming-pools fed by water from the springs).

 Even a complete novice can be confident of hooking a gigantic Nile perch. But such good fortune for an angler naturally has its price – you must pay for a licence and for the boat and hire of fishing-tackle. The Oasis Club also lays claim to any fish caught, having customers for them in Nairobi.

 Showers in the palm grove.

About 20 km north of Loyangalani the *El Molo,* Africa's smallest tribe, have their village. Not so long ago these people survived almost exclusively on the fish they speared and trapped. Nowadays they live to a large extent off tourists taking photographs. The El Molo suffer from a bone disease (presumably brought on by drinking the mineral-rich lake water). Years ago they seemed threatened with extinction but their numbers have risen again, from 200 to 500.

**Mount Kulal** (2,290 m), an extinct volcano split in two by a 1,200-m-long fissure, is reached from Loyangalani by way of a boneshaking track. No one has yet crossed the razor-sharp ridge between its north and south peaks.

### East Turkana National Park

From Loyangalani the road leads north into an increasingly lifeless and strange landscape. In the East Turkana National Park (Sibiloi National Park) lies the *Koobi Fora* fossil-site where in 1972 Richard Leakey discovered the skull of *Homo habilis*, who lived there 1.5 million years ago. (Driving up to the park is really only for the intrepid.)

Well before Koobi Fora the route for the less adventurous branches off to North Horr, 36 km from the turn-off.

**North Horr,** an oasis on the edge of the Chalbi Desert, has very little in the way of vegetation. During the dry season the Gabbra, a nomadic people, gather around the watering-places with their cattle. There is a mission and a school run by German missionaries.

**The Chalbi Desert** is actually a dried-out lake bed, flat as a pancake and extending beyond the horizon. So intense are the mirages produced by the shimmering heat that you seem to be encircled by great stretches of water. Under no circumstances leave the track; it is impossible to find your bearings here. With the onset of the rainy season, the Chalbi can turn into a genuine sea. It then becomes impassable for months, to be transformed afterwards into a miracle of grass and flowers.

**Marsabit** (alt. 1,400 m; pop. 10,000), a mountain mass reaching 2,000 m in height, with dense forests and (most important of all) fresh water, draws people from all over the otherwise arid region. Its game reserve is scenically one of the most exceptional places in Kenya. Nomadic Rendille, Boran and Gabbra tribesmen are among those to be found stocking up with vital supplies.

**Marsabit Game Reserve:** The volcanic massif is dotted with truly romantic crater lakes, including one known as *Lake Paradise*. Marsabit's elephants are famous for their unusually large tusks (they can weigh more than 50 kg).

 *Marsabit Lodge.*

The drive from Marsabit to Isiolo (227 km) has to be made in convoy – vehicles assemble every other day. From Isiolo return to Nairobi via the main road through Nanyuki, Nyeri and Thika.

## To the west side of Lake Turkana

Heading for the west side of Lake Turkana, the road north is mostly already tarmacked, and further work is in progress. Leaving Nairobi, the route is again via Naivasha and Nakuru. From Nakuru you drive through forested uplands to Eldoret.

**Eldoret** (312 km from Nairobi; alt. 2,100 m; pop. 55,000): This burgeoning trading centre stands in the middle of what was once European-settled farmland. A new hotel should help Eldoret to establish itself as a base for trips round and about.

 *Sirikwa Hotel.*

**Kitale** (380 km from Nairobi; alt. 1,890 m; pop. 31,000) was once the epitome of a European settlers' country town. Today it is the centre of the fruit-growing industry (apples). Its brightly coloured and sometimes lovingly painted houses are worth stopping to have a look at.

*Mount Elgon*, designated one of Kenya's national parks, rises west of Kitale. The volcano's 4,324-m main summit, however, is actually in Uganda. During the rains in April and May and again in August and September the mountain is virtually inaccessible.

 *Mount Elgon Lodge.*

The *Cherangani Hills* to the north-east of Kitale are scenically very attractive, with strange, high-moorland vegetation (the hills even so are not a conservation area). The road, the main route into the Sudan, runs straight northwards via Kapenguria and Sigor.

About 320 km beyond Kitale you arrive in Lodwar, administrative capital of the Turkana district, with a mission (filling station!), police station and prison, in which Jomo Kenyatta was interned for two years. From Lodwar a road runs to Lake Turkana's western shore, rather less hostile than its eastern one. Endless sand dunes clad with palms extend along the lakeside.

 *Lake Turkana Fishing Lodge* in Ferguson's Gulf; *Fishing Lodge* in Eliya Springs (very simple).

# Lake Victoria

Had the British not shown the overwhelming interest they did in Lake Victoria, Kenya would probably never have become a British colony. Fed by a fever of 19th c. exploration, the drive to control the headwaters of the Nile became a matter of the utmost prestige.

Excitement over the sources of the Nile died down long ago, and with it the passionate interest in Lake Victoria, which subsequently ceased to be on the tourist track. The time has now gone, though, when a holidaymaker's choice was limited to the coast and the game reserves. For anyone who has seen enough of animals and has the urge to get to know the country and its people, a trip to Lake Victoria offers a real glimpse into how the majority of Kenyans live. This is no journey into a photogenic past; it is a trip into the vigorous, living present of a young nation.

Follow the A 104 from Nairobi through Limuru and Naivasha to Nakuru (see page 70). At the exit to the town, take the tarmacked C 56 on the left. Impressive farms border the road on either side. Between Elburgon and Molo there are stretches of dark forest with herds of sheep grazing at their edges. (Molo lamb appears on almost every menu.)

Turn left in Mau Summit on to the good B 1 in the direction of Kericho. On the left-hand side as you drive along the road are the spurs of *Mau Forest,* the largest forested area in Kenya. Then ahead the shining, light-green tea-fields of Kericho come into sight.

**Kericho** Alt. 1,830 m; pop. 30,000
Kericho (266 km from Nairobi) is Kenya's tea-growing centre. The land around is ideally suited to tea. It is high-lying and sees a great deal of sunshine, yet a shower of rain falls nearly every day.

The seemingly endless fields of tea-bushes look as if they have just been freshly mown at hip height. For four years the bushes, which otherwise can grow up to 9 m tall, will have been cut back sufficiently often to keep them small and make them yield well. In this way they stay productive for up to sixty years. The pickers, wearing thick rubber aprons to protect them from the hard twigs, harvest only the leaves at the tips of the young shoots. The leaves then have to be thoroughly processed.

Kenyan tea is of excellent quality. The country is the third largest tea-exporter in the world after Sri Lanka and India.

Kericho is surrounded by large tea-plantations, each of which permanently employs 500 pickers. To the south of the town, the tea-fields become smaller. These belong to individual farmers who join together to form a co-operative.

 *Kericho Tea Hotel* (very pleasant and quiet) on the edge of the tea-fields.

**Sotik** (306 km from Nairobi) is the centre of a passion-fruit growing area. From it a dirt road branches off to the *Masai Mara Game Reserve* (see page 65).

**Kisii** (365 km from Nairobi; alt. 1,880; pop. 35,000) is located in the most densely populated part of Kenya. It is from here that the soapstone comes that is carved into the animals and figures found in souvenir shops the length and breadth of the country.

The road continues through Migori, an old gold-mining town, to Tanzania. Some

25 km beyond Kisii, however, a very good road off to the right leads to *Homa Bay* on Lake Victoria.

**Homa Bay** is gearing itself to take advantage of the abundance of fish in the world's third largest lake. Nearby is the *Lambwe Valley National Park,* home of a rare species of antelope – though unfortunately of the tsetse fly too.

 *Homa Bay Hotel*, by the ferry.

## Lake Victoria Alt. 1,130 m

The lake, which was named after Queen Victoria, is 78 m at its deepest, has an area of 68,000 sq km, and flows into the White Nile. It is not a suitable place for bathing, being infested with the bilharzia fluke in addition to being a paradise for crocodile and hippo.

Some day its vast reservoir of water could become more important than its wealth of fish. A scheme has already been advanced for the construction of a pipe-line to irrigate Kenya's semi-arid regions. Political and financial considerations still for the moment bar the way, but the project brings a completely new dimension to the battle against hunger in Africa. There are no luxury cruises on Lake Victoria nowadays, as there used to be in colonial times. But international navigation on the lake will probably revive, especially in view of the fact that in 1983 the countries of the former East African Community (Kenya, Tanzania, Uganda) pledged themselves to greater co-operation. The islands of *Rabuor* and *Ndere* may one day be developed for tourism.

From *Homa Bay* you can either take the ferry to *Kisumu* or drive there on the dirt road skirting the lake's eastern side (caution is necessary in rain). The scenery is rather boring and the view of the lake is obscured by the islands, making it impossible to appreciate just how sea-like it is. The *Luo settlements* are interesting, however (the Luo are Kenya's second largest tribe). Some of the reed-covered mud huts are attractively decorated with earth pigment.

**Kisumu** 410 km; pop. 160,000

Kisumu, third largest city in Kenya and unofficial capital of the Luo (Luo means

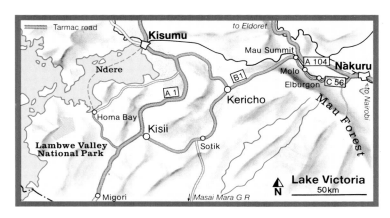

'swamp'), is yet another city that owes its existence to the Mombasa–Kampala railway.

The Kenyan government is increasing its efforts to develop Lake Victoria economically, and to open the lake to tourism. A second hotel has recently been completed. But the *Sunset Hotel*, from the terrace of which you can watch the gloriously coloured sunsets, is still the place to stay.

 *Sunset Hotel; Imperial Hotel.*

 Mombasa to Nairobi and Kisumu.

# Excursions into Tanzania

In Tanzania tourism has not been developed to anything like the same extent as in Kenya. Even the fairly modest steps taken in that direction were largely halted for seven years by closure of the border between the two. Although with international help an effort is now being made to redevelop a tourist infrastructure, Tanzania's holiday facilities cannot hope to measure up to Kenya's for a considerable time to come. Still, as long as you are prepared to pay for relatively little in the way of comfort and nothing very special in the way of food, you can enjoy the unspoiled loveliness of Tanzania's parks and reserves.

If you plan to visit Tanzania, you must obtain the necessary visa from your Tanzanian embassy before setting out. There are regular scheduled air services from Nairobi to both Dar-es-Salaam and the less frequently used Kilimanjaro International Airport (for Arusha). On entering Tanzania by car, you must pay vehicle duty at the frontier. If the car has been hired in Kenya, there is also the problem of insurance cover – the policy will not be valid for driving in Tanzania. Within Tanzania, safaris are arranged by a number of operators. Remember that all services must be paid for in foreign currency (sterling, US dollars) even if you book in Kenya.

Tanzania's main tourist attractions are concentrated in the area from Kilimanjaro westwards to Lake Victoria (see map page 28). So if you are driving from Nairobi, the route is the same as if heading for Amboseli Park – the A 104 via Kajiado to the border town of Namanga. (Do not rely on being able to fill up again in Namanga. Petrol-hungry Tanzanians often empty the Namanga filling stations.) From Namanga it is 112 km to Arusha, on a good tarmac road.

**Arusha** (pop. 60,000) is the major town of northern Tanzania and has acquired a world-wide reputation as a venue for international conferences. The famous Amboseli meerschaum, used for carving pipe-bowls and figurines, comes from nearby and will be seen on sale. Arusha is the starting-point for all safaris inside Tanzania.

 *Mount Meru Hotel; Mount Meru Lodge.*

**Arusha National Park** is located immediately to the north of the town and includes the volcanic Mount Meru massif (4,566 m). Except for lion, virtually every kind of East African animal is established here. If you intend to climb the summit, be sure to take a guide.

**Ngurdoto National Park** is almost continuous with the east side of Arusha Park. It incorporates the Ngurdoto crater and Lake Momella, the latter well-known from having appeared on film.

 *Lake Momella Lodge.*

*The Ngorongoro Crater*

**Kilimanjaro Game Reserve** is 130 km from Arusha along the Moshi road. The 17,000-sq-km reserve takes in the whole of the huge volcanic plug above a height of 1,800 m. Elephant, buffalo, antelope and rhino frequent the mountain forests. Above the tree-line, the landscape is typically Afro-alpine, with giant lobelia and heathers. Kilimanjaro has two summits: the Dolomite-like Mawenzi (5,151 m) and the permanently ice-capped Uhuru Peak (formerly Kibo, 5,895 m).

 Climbing Uhuru Peak requires no mountaineering ability, but you do need to be exceptionally fit and to have purpose-designed clothing for protection against the cold you will experience at such great heights.

An expedition from *Marangu* takes five days in all — 3½ days up, 1½ days down. About 15 km are covered daily, the nights being spent in simple huts. Although the slow climb allows the body some time to acclimatise to the altitude, many people find they literally have no breath for the last lap. You are strongly advised to take medical advice before embarking on the climb and you should descend immediately at the first sign of altitude sickness. The hotels in Marangu organise the climbs, complete with guides, porters and equipment.

 *Kibo Hotel; Marangu Hotel.*

**Lake Manyara National Park** (650 sq km, 102 km west of Arusha) is a famous paradise for waterfowl. It is also known for its 'tree lions' — perfectly ordinary lions with a habit of taking their siesta in the fork of a tree.

*Lake Manyara Hotel.*

**Ngorongoro,** (6,500 sq km) is unquestionably Tanzania's most spectacular game conservation area. With a diameter of 20 km, the Ngorongoro is

*The Serengeti*

the second biggest crater in the world. The crater bottom – 600 m below the 2,400-m-high rim – is home to an unusually large concentration of East African game animals, including elephant, lion, rhino, hippo, antelope, different kinds of gazelle, wildebeest and zebra, while on *Lake Magadi* there are populations of flamingos, storks and herons. The crater bottom is accessible only to vehicles with four-wheel drive. A 1.75-million-year-old skull discovered in the *Olduvai Gorge,* north-west of the crater, proves that man has lived here from the very earliest times. Grouped around the Ngorongoro are a number of other craters, some of them over 3,000 m high. They include Oldeani, Olmoti, Embagai and the Loolmalassin Hills.

 *Ngorongoro Wildlife Lodge*, on the crater rim, and *Ngorongoro Crater Lodge.* (Land Rovers can be hired; airstrip for light aircraft.)

Near the Wildlife Lodge there is a stone commemorating Michael Grzimek, who was killed in 1959 when his plane crashed in the crater.

**Serengeti National Park** (13,000 sq km), giant among Tanzania's parks, was first brought to Europe's attention by Professor Bernhard Grzimek (who wrote *Serengeti shall not die*). It forms a single natural unit with the Masai Mara, and like the Mara is the scene of the great wildebeest migration. Impressive as this event is to witness, it has the disadvantage that at certain times of year the reserves seem almost empty of game. Generally speaking the animals migrate north to Kenya in June, when there is water to be had there; they travel south again to drier Tanzania from November onwards.

🛏 *Seronera Lodge; Lobo Lodge.*

**Ex** ✈ **Zanzibar:** There are daily flights from Mombasa to Zanzibar. The day-trip includes a guided tour of the spice fields.

ℹ Air Tanzania, Nairobi, PO Box 20077, tel. 33 62 24 and 33 63 97; UTC, Mombasa, tel. 31 63 33.

# Useful words and phrases

A handful of Swahili words will not of course go very far, but it helps to know a few, in particular the greetings.

| | |
|---|---|
| Harambee | Together we will succeed (the country's motto) |
| uhuru | freedom |
| jambo | hello |
| habari? | how are you? |
| mzuri (*on the coast also* salama *or* njema) | good (it would be terribly impolite to start by complaining!) |
| hakuna matata | no problem (is used continuously) |
| pole | sorry |
| pole pole | slowly (it can't be said often enough to safari bus-drivers) |
| karibu | welcome |
| kwa heri | goodbye (literally 'with luck') |
| asante (sana) | thank you (very much) |
| tafadhali | please |
| bwana | Mr |
| bibi | Mrs |
| mzee | respectful form of address for an older man |
| mama | the same for an older woman. |

| | | | |
|---|---|---|---|
| baado | not yet | maziwa | milk |
| baadaye | later | moto | warm |
| sasa | now | baridi | cold |
| leo | today | kali | hot (spicy) |
| kesho | tomorrow | pesa | money |
| ninataka | I would like | bei gani? | how dear? |
| sitaki | I don't want | ghali | expensive |
| kahawa | coffee | rahisi | cheap |
| chai | tea (also a tip) | watoto | children |
| kula | to eat | jumaa | family |
| kunywa | to drink | nyumba | house |
| kulala | to sleep | manyatta | Masai hut |
| kununua | to buy | shamba | field |
| rafiki | friend | chafu | dirty |
| jua | sun | safi | clean |
| mvua | rain | | |
| bahari | ocean | | |

| | | | | | |
|---|---|---|---|---|---|
| samaki | fish | 1 | moja | 9 | tisa |
| maji | water | 2 | mbili | 10 | kumi |
| sukari | sugar | 3 | tatu | 11 | kumi na moja |
| chumvi | salt | 4 | nne | 12 | kumi na mbili |
| nyama | meat | 5 | tano | 20 | ishirini |
| wanyama | animals | 6 | sitsa | 50 | hamsini |
| matunda | fruit | 7 | saba | 100 | mia |
| mboga | vegetables | 8 | nane | | |

# Useful things to know

## Before you go
### Climate and the rainy seasons

The climate is certainly one of Kenya's greatest attractions. Although the equator passes through the country, large areas nevertheless escape the usual disadvantages of the tropics. In the highlands, the climate (in Nairobi, for example) is one of the pleasantest in the world. Even during January to March – the hottest time of the year, when the maximum temperature reaches 28°C – it cools down to 14°C at night. In the cooler months (June to August) nighttime temperatures drop as low as 5°C.

In Mombasa the highest temperatures vary between 28°C (June to August) and 32°C (January to March), while night-time averages do not fall below 21°C. Whether these temperatures feel uncomfortable depends on the humidity.

Being on the equator, Kenya has far less seasonal variation than Europe or North America. Only the two rainy periods make any difference to the tourist season. The 'short rains' (mid-November to mid-December) are hardly a problem because the rain falls largely at night. The 'long rains' (April to June), on the other hand, can be unpleasant, with many days of heavy rain. With changes of climate affecting the entire continent, even in Kenya the rains cannot wholly be relied upon. April can quite well turn out dry, and in the dry season it can sometimes rain.

### Clothes

On the coast even light summer clothes can often prove too warm. That is why the local *kangas* and *kikois* are so favoured. During the cooler months (May to August) you might occasionally have use for a lightweight jacket. Plastic sandals are a must for the beach.

On safari you will need strong shoes. Although the 'safari-look' is 'in' and khaki clothes are on sale everywhere, jeans are just as practical – but they do tend to be hot during the day. The higher the altitude of your safari destination, though, the more advisable it is to have a warm jacket. (A plastic raincoat can be useful too.) Generally speaking dress in hotels is informal (a few exclusive clubs excepted). You can usually manage without a jacket and tie. After dusk, however, beach clothes and shorts are not regarded as suitable.

Whether on the beach or on safari, a sun-hat and sun-glasses are vital.

### Getting to Kenya

Daily air services link Kenya with Europe. Most of the scheduled flights go to Nairobi, the charter flights to Mombasa. The journey time from London is eight hours. An airport tax is levied on departure from Kenya.

There are direct flights (16 hours) from New York to West Africa, and thence on to Nairobi with possible stops on the way.

### Immigration and customs

Kenyan Customs will not look twice at the usual kind of luggage, including up to 0.7 litres of alcohol, a carton of cigarettes and normal photographic equipment. But if you have more than two cameras or an unusual number of accessories, you may be required to leave a deposit, to be reclaimed when you take them out again (the same goes for video recorders and surf boards, to prevent unauthorised imports). If you are determined to take ivory jewellery to Kenya, make sure you declare it on entry and obtain a certificate so as to avoid problems when leaving. It is pointless to take fresh fruit or cut flowers; not only is it carrying coals to Newcastle but they will simply be confiscated anyway.

Firearms must be declared of course; and the Kenyans do not want drugs in their country either.

Almost anything can be taken out of Kenya except ivory, game trophies, skins, snail and sea shells, foreign currency not previously imported, and Kenyan shillings.

## Luggage

On charter flights 20 kg is the limit and excess luggage is not allowed even on payment of a surcharge. Leave space for souvenirs – you do not need a 'wardrobe' in Africa and all the hotels have a laundry service. Do not pack any pressurised sprays in your suitcase as they could burst during the flight.

## Travel documents

Visitors from the UK travelling as tourists and not planning to stay longer than three months require a passport valid for at least three months beyond the date of entry. If a visa for South Africa is already entered in the passport, a visa for Kenya must be obtained from the Kenyan Embassy (see page 94).

US citizens require visas in addition to passports; contact the Kenyan Embassy (see page 94).

## Vaccinations

At the moment people entering Kenya direct from Europe or the US do not require proof of inoculation. Those who arrive via other African countries, or who intend to visit Tanzania, generally need certificates of vaccination against yellow fever and cholera. These regulations change frequently, so it is essential to make enquiries about the current state of affairs before you leave.

A gamma globulin injection against hepatitis is advisable. You are also very strongly advised to take a course of malaria tablets. Malaria is on the increase again in East Africa and there is at present no complete protection against it. For a stay of up to four weeks you would probably be recommended to take *Lariam* (1 tablet a week, commencing the week before departure and finishing a week after you return). For longer stays *Resochin* (2 tablets a week commencing a week before departure and finishing four weeks after you return). You should carry *Fansidar* with you, to be taken in the event of a high fever (3 tablets once only, in addition to the *Resochin*). If you develop a high temperature after your return home – even if it is weeks later – tell your doctor that you have been in Kenya.

Malaria is transmitted through the bite of the anopheles mosquito, which becomes active after nightfall. It is then advisable to keep yourself covered as much as possible, in light-coloured clothing, and to apply an insect repellent to any exposed parts of the body.

Up-to-date information can be obtained from the School of Tropical Medicine in London (see page 94).

## What to take
### Medical and first-aid kit

Your medical kit should include any medicines you ordinarily have to take. In addition you should have with you something to prevent malaria, something for sunburn and insect bites, headache tablets and anything else you anticipate needing, such as ear-drops. It is also important to include something for treating diarrhoea.

The food in larger hotels can be trusted, but avoid having a lot of cold drinks. As far as *bilharzia* is concerned, there is only one remedy, namely to completely avoid slow-flowing rivers and freshwater lakes. Tourists going on safari should add to their list plasters, an elastic bandage, iodine and antiseptic cream. Good, reasonably priced insecticide sprays for use indoors or in tents can be bought in Kenya.

## Cosmetics, miscellaneous

The selection available in hotel boutiques varies, so it is best to take all the cosmetics you will need with you from home. You are likely in Kenya to use more suntan cream (buy one with a high protection factor!) and more films than usual. And do not forget to take some holiday reading.

## Photography and films

Take sufficient supplies of film and photographic materials with you from home. They are expensive in Kenya and film of the correct ASA number may not always be available. You also need covers to protect your equipment from dust and heat when on safari.

If you do not already have a telescopic lens, you should seriously think about acquiring one for Kenya. Even if safari buses do take you close to the animals, photos shot from a distance are often the best. Remember that with a telescopic lens you need a more sensitive film (at least 200 ASA) — stalking the animals often means going deep into semi-shade.

# During your stay

## Accommodation

A good hotel in Kenya can be expected to match European standards. The low prices charged by the cheap hotels on the coast and the so-called Local Guesthouses inland, on the other hand, are an indication that too much should not be expected of them. Safari hotels are known as 'lodges'. Most are bungalow-

style but otherwise no different from a high-class hotel. 'Tented camps' are a Kenyan speciality and will appeal to anyone hankering after the splendours of an old-style safari. Two, or if need be three, beds fit comfortably into the luxurious high-walled tents. There is a place to sit in front of the tent and a large 'bathroom' with roomy shower. Food in the central restaurant is equal to that of a top-class hotel. This means you do not have to have a boy-scout mentality to experience being that little bit closer to nature and listening to the sounds of the African night separated only by the walls of a tent. There are tented camps in or near almost all the national parks.

## Car hire

In Mombasa, Malindi and Nairobi cars can be hired from all the well-known rental companies as well as from local firms. Either way the condition of the vehicles often leaves a lot to be desired. Rates vary a great deal and it pays to shop around (watch out for extras!). Normally the driver must be between 23 and 70 and have held a driving licence for at least two years (an international licence is not required). Most hire-firms demand payment in advance.

The condition of the roads also varies considerably. New stretches are constantly being built; but just as continuously relatively new roads are destroyed by violent rain storms and too heavy traffic. To finance the upkeep of roads the Kenyans have introduced tolls on the major routes.

## Currency

The official unit of currency is the Kenyan shilling (Ksh) = 100 cents. Unofficially people still reckon in the old Kenyan pound (= 20 Ksh). There are coins of 5, 10 and 50 cents and 1 and 5 shillings, and banknotes of 10, 20, 50, 100, 200 and 500 shillings.

Current exchange rates can be found in the national press, or obtained from banks.

There is no limit to the amount of foreign currency you can take into Kenya. A foreign currency declaration must be completed on arrival and a receipt obtained from the bank or hotel used for each subsequent exchange transaction. On departure your foreign currency declaration will be checked. The import or export of Kenyan currency is strictly forbidden. It is best for tourists and holidaymakers to take most of the money needed for their trip in sterling travellers' cheques. Any bank or international hotel will accept them. Not every hotel (lodge) in Kenya does, though, and on longer safaris you should ensure you take sufficient in Kenyan shillings.

## Electricity

The voltage is 230–240 volts AC but in practice is also suitable for 220-volt appliances. A three-prong adaptor is required. Many lodges have generators that are switched off after 11 or 12 at night, after which paraffin lamps are used instead.

## Group travel or independent?

Whether you travel independently or in a group is a matter of temperament. In theory there is no problem about exploring Kenya by making your own arrangements. In practice, however, difficulties can arise. Unless you have friends or relatives there, it can become very complicated and very costly arranging the holiday from outside the country. If you leave arrangements to be made 'on the spot', in peak season you may find it too late and all the hotels fully booked.

The price advantages of group travel are also not to be underestimated. In any case the range of choice available offers individualists a chance to compromise. If a group of fifteen seems too big, you can perhaps opt for a group of four.

## Insurance

It is important to have adequate insurance cover against medical expenses and loss or theft of luggage and personal effects. Insurance can usually be arranged through your tour operator.

## Newspapers

The *Standard, Daily Nation* and the *Kenya Times* are English-language newspapers, as are the *Weekly Review* and the *Coast Week*. Foreign newspapers and magazines arrive late and are expensive.

## Opening times

*Banks:* Mondays to Fridays 9 am–2 pm. Do not change money on the black market – there is little advantage, people are often cheated, and you risk prison if caught.

*Shops:* Most are open from 9 am to 6 pm (Saturdays to 1 pm). But in shopping centres and bazaars they often stay open longer, including Sundays and holidays.

## Post and telephone

Stamps are obtainable at post offices and large hotels.

International phone calls are best made from main post offices. Dial 0196 for the international operator. International direct dialling is now increasingly available.

Post offices are usually open on weekdays from 8 am–1 pm and 2–4.30 or 5 pm; some larger ones also open on Saturdays.

## Tipping
There are countries in which tips are demanded a lot more insistently than in Kenya, so all the more reason for not forgetting to tip. There are no hard and fast rules. The driver who has quartered the bush with you for a week and enlightened you about the animals deserves at least 350 Ksh. A quarter of that would be about right for the waiter and 'room boy'.

## Transport in Kenya
Bus is the cheapest way to travel but will not suit everybody. If you take a taxi you should agree the fare in advance because only a few have meters. Journeys between Mombasa and the hotels are very expensive (prices are given in the hotels).

A first-class train ticket from Mombasa to Nairobi includes bed linen, supper and breakfast.

# Important addresses
## Tour operators
In Mombasa, and even more in Nairobi, there are a large number of tour operators either offering the standard tours or catering for special requirements. Recommended for English-speaking tourists:

*Pollman's Tours & Safaris*
**Mombasa**
Moi Ave
PO Box 84 198
tel. 31 25 65–7

**Nairobi**
Cannon House
PO Box 45 895
tel. 33 79 52

## Tourist information offices
**In UK**
*Kenya Tourist Office*
25 New Bond St
London W14 9HD
tel. 071 355 3144

**In US**
*Kenya Tourist Office*
424 Madison Ave
New York NY 10017
tel. 212 486 1300

**In Kenya**
*Ministry of Tourism and Wildlife*
PO Box 30 027, Nairobi

*Mombasa Tourist Association*
Moi Ave, Mombasa

## Diplomatic offices
**In UK**
*Kenyan Embassy*
45 Portland Place
London W1N 4AS
tel. 071 636 2371

**In US**
*Kenyan Embassy*
2249 R St NW
Washington DC 20008
tel. 202 387 6101

**In Kenya (Nairobi)**
*British Embassy*
Bruce House
Standard St
PO Box 30465; tel. 335944

*US Embassy*
Moi Ave
PO Box 30137; tel. 334141

*Australian Embassy*
Development House
Moi Ave
PO Box 30360; tel. 334666

*Canadian Embassy*
Comcraft House
Haile Selassie Ave
PO Box 30481; tel. 334033

## Health
Hospital for Tropical Diseases
4 St Pancras Way
London NW1
tel. 071 387 4411

# Index

NP = National Park; GR = Game Reserve; NR = National Reserve.

Original German text: Heidegret Klöter. Translation: Wendy Bell
Series editor, English edition: Jane Rolph

© Verlag Robert Pfützner GmbH, München. Original German edition

© Jarrold Publishing, Norwich, Great Britain 1/91. English language edition worldwide

Published in the US and Canada by Hunter Publishing, Inc.,
300 Raritan Center Parkway, Edison NJ 08818

Illustrations: J. Allan Cash Ltd pages 17, 50, 70, 79; J. Davis Travel Photography pages 46, 55, 57, 71, 73; S. Johnson pages 19, 56, 63, 69, 78 (top and bottom right); Kenya National Tourist Office page 25 (both); R. Lake pages 29, 53, 66, 76, 78 (top and bottom left); K. Rowe pages 26, 41, 62; Miss M. Tracey pages 1, 3, 22; G. Webb page 58; World Pictures page 68; D. Yardy pages 4, 9, 19, 23, 38, 45, 59 (both), 61, 64, 87, 88.

The publishers have made every endeavour to ensure the accuracy of this publication but can accept no responsibility for any errors or omissions. They would, however, appreciate notification of any inaccuracies to correct future editions.

Printed in Italy

ISBN 0–7117–0486–4